OUT OF STEP

A MEMOIR

ANTHONY MOLL

MAD CREEK BOOKS, AN IMPRINT OF
THE OHIO STATE UNIVERSITY PRESS
COLUMBUS

Names: Moll, Anthony (Writer and educator), author.
Title: Out of step : a memoir / Anthony Moll.
Description: Columbus : Mad Creek Books, an imprint of The Ohio State
    University Press, [2018] | Includes bibliographical references. | Winner
    of the 2017 The Ohio State University Press "The Journal" Non/Fiction
    Prize
Identifiers: LCCN 2018003872 | ISBN 9780814254820 (pbk. ; alk. paper)
    | ISBN 0814254829 (pbk. ; alk. paper)
Subjects: LCSH: Moll, Anthony (Writer and educator) | Bisexual men—
    Biography. | Gay military personnel—United States.
Classification: LCC HQ74.73.M65 A3 2018 | DDC 306.76/50811—dc23
LC record available at https://lccn.loc.gov/2018003872

Cover design by Regina Starace
Text design by Juliet Williams
Type set in Adobe Sabon LT Std

For queer folks who run away from home.

CONTENTS

Acknowledgments   ix

A Note on the Text   xi

MARKS   1

PHOTO: CHILDREN ARDENT FOR SOME DESPERATE GLORY   11

WHAT SEPTEMBER LEFT   15

HEADLINES FROM THE *RENO-GAZETTE JOURNAL*
THE MORNING OF SEPTEMBER 11, 2001   21

WRONG AS TWO BOYS, PT. I   23

MUSCLE MEMORY   37

GREAT BASIN   43

BACHELOR ENLISTED QUARTERS, CAMP CARROLL, KOREA   50

PHOTO: MK 19   54

PLUCKY AND DUMB   57

WRONG AS TWO BOYS, PT. II   61

SISTERS IN THE PRESENCE OF STRANGERS, PT. I   70

PHOTO: CEDANT ARMA TOGAE   78

ON RITUAL   81

PHOTO: CLUB SPOT   91

MY SIDE OF THE FENCE   95

PAGEANT   104

CASUALTIES   111

PHOTO: SLICK SLEEVES   114

DOGS OF WAR   118

PHOTO: DRESSED UP   127

LAST YEAR   130

GOING OUT   139

PHOTO: PRIDE, 2011   143

SISTERS IN THE PRESENCE OF STRANGERS, PT. II   147

PHOTO: WESTWARD   152

Notes   155

ACKNOWLEDGMENTS

I WANT TO THANK everyone from these organizations, institutions, and publications for sharing, strengthening, or loving this work in its early stages:

A section of this book was submitted as an MFA Thesis at University of Baltimore.

An earlier version of "Going Out" appeared in the Winter 2013 issue of *Gertrude*.

An earlier version of "Pageant" appeared in the 2015 issue of *Welter*.

An earlier version of "My Side of the Fence" appeared in the anthology *Plorkology*.

An earlier version of "Last Year" and "MK 19" appeared in the anthology *Incoming* and was recorded for KPBS San Diego by So Say We All.

Part of this manuscript was developed while attending the Marlboro College Summer Writing Intensive coordinated by Marlboro College and Words After War.

Thank you also to the various mentors and educators who have helped to strengthen me as a writer and thinker in order to make this book possible, and thank you to everyone who helped to build this work at some point in its adolescence. My thanks also go out to Michael Kardos for selecting this book for the 2017 Non/Fiction prize, and to the entire team at *The Journal* and Mad Creek Books at The Ohio State University Press for helping me to bring the book to life.

Finally, thank you to all my friends and lovers who made this book happen, both in the years discussed here and in the period it took to write it.

A NOTE ON THE TEXT

THIS BOOK is a work of creative nonfiction, but like any collection of memories, written or recalled, it is likely to contain inconsistencies, contradictions or outright errors. I didn't make anything up, but I didn't write everything down either. Some names were changed, some weren't.

MARKS

I GREW UP with the same mythologies as other dumb American boys.

Yet when I picture a statue of David, I do not imagine Michelangelo's seventeen-foot-tall marble masterpiece. The milky figure is a breathtaking study in masculine form, but this sculpted nude has never seemed to fit my image of the young David who left the tending of his father's sheep and faced the warrior Goliath. He's too beautiful, too fully formed. This David is not the youngest child of Saul. This David is a young *man*: a college quarterback, an Olympic swimmer.

Now, Donatello's David: that's my David. Donatello gives us an effeminate and delicate boy, hand on his hip like some bratty bottom. He is shown just after the battle—Goliath's severed head at his feet, beard exfoliating David's toes—but it's easy to see that this sculpture shows a boy at the brink. Rather than Christ-like abs, the bronze David wears a boyish paunch and effeminate hips. His body appears soft, his demeanor, gentle and shy. He seems nymphic, right leg tilted almost coquettishly. One of the wings from Goliath's great helmet creeps up the back of David's leg, stopping just shy of where the curve of his backside meets his thighs. The whole scene seems so boyish and queer that even art historians recognize its homoerotic qualities. This unmarked body, not yet sculpted by hardship, a girlish boy mixed up in someone else's war by folly and by a childish pride: that's my David.

I'd like to say I joined the military unmarked, that I arrived at the Military Entrance Processing Station, a multipurpose facility that acts as everything from a clinic for physical exams to an administrative office for processing those entering the military, as young and pure as a Renaissance bronze. Yet the truth of my enlistment is that the physician inspecting my young body with latex gloves missed neither the tiny scar on my forehead where I had fallen from top bunk onto a Tonka truck as a child, nor the dime-sized Mongolian Blue Spot decorating my backside. Still, aside from these minor blemishes, my young, soft body raised a hand and swore the oath of enlistment without any real damage at eighteen years.

Teeth

The first mark came early. As my platoon huddled together, celebrating a well-run obstacle course in the middle of our basic-training experience, a helmet-clad head jerked back toward my face, sending a good portion of my front teeth to the back of my throat.

Basic training being the frenzied experience that it is, the emergency dentist at the clinic asked if I was experiencing any sensitivity in the injured teeth. Me being in no pain and terrified of the backlash of my drill sergeants should I miss training, I insisted I felt fine, and walked around for the remainder of basic training, and several weeks that followed, looking like Lloyd Christmas.

Eyebrow

I crawled slowly through the Southern California hills, avoiding the ridgeline and staying low to the ground in my foliage-decorated ghille suit. *Slow is fast,* I repeated in my head, a mantra of the week's training. I found my spot slowly. Deployed the rifle slowly. Took slow aim. Breathe. Breathe. Breathe. Squeeze. The sniper rifle cracked sharply. The scope, mounted atop the receiver, snapped back with it, marking me with what my comrades will later call *a kiss*. I felt only the slightest tickle on my brow as the weapon recoiled in my hands, and then, as though a slow rain had begun without my notice, a wet stream crawled its way down my face. Unaware of any injury, I finished the exercise. Target. Breathe. Squeeze. Target. Breathe. Squeeze. Target. These are what matter when one is shooting.

When I returned, my grass-adorned helmet in one hand and the rifle in another, one of our trainers pointed the injury out to me.

"Whooooeey! Looks like she gave you a little *kiss* on your forehead. Come over here and let's get you cleaned up."

My hand touched my face, and returned covered in camouflage paint and red. Her kiss would leave a scar visible for years.

Hips

I read an essay recently that reminded radicals that we mustn't forget the history of appropriation and imperialism present in tattoos. The idea referred both to the recent tradition of tattoos of foreign languages on the bodies of westerners, and to how tattooing was introduced to the West: through Captain James Cook's exploration of the South Pacific, and through the spread of the U.S. military.

As a young American soldier in Seoul a decade earlier, I thought of neither of these fitting connections as a friend and I stumbled toward a back-alley shop near what troops called "Hooker Hill," a brightly lit alley where Korean and Russian women call out to passersby from the doors of dimly lit bars.

"Mister, I know you."

As we entered the shop just at the hill's base, the middle-aged Korean owner and artist quickly recognized me and my friend Danyel as Americans and as soldiers. We were swiftly seated, and as we fingered through the folders of bright illustrations, the artist, clad in a Rolling Stones tee, pointed at the wrapped needles he held.

"Clean. American. First use."

We agreed on a price, the shop minimum, and he began to set up his station.

"I lock the door," he insisted as he pulled the bolt lock shut, the legal status of tattoos being gray in the country generally, but entirely off limits for U.S. soldiers.

This sounds familiar, I know: cliché even. It's eerie how traditions like this, like soldiers getting drunk in a foreign country and getting a tattoo, repeat themselves, how young men and women mimic cultural fables. In the morning, as a shower trickled over my hungover head, I glanced down at my first tattoo, my queer tattoo. I had eschewed the anchors, pinups, and eagles that so many soldiers of my period receive, accepting instead a flaming star, just below the waistline on my taut hip. The star was something slightly off, something a bit feminine, something hidden.

Hands

I don't belong here. The Baltimore Veterans Affairs Hospital is for old men. Veterans with mesh caps with Korea or Vietnam emblazoned across them. Broken men. Worn bodies. A thin man in camouflage pants wheels an oxygen tank behind him. A thick man showing off his tattooed arms coughs a wet cough into a towel.

I wish I could say that I shattered both of my hands doing something heroic. How might a warrior injure himself? Charging a hill? Shrapnel? Gulf War Syndrome maybe, tiny desert sands stirred with weaponized chemicals. Damp jungle air mixed with defoliating herbicides.

In my early twenties, I broke my hands skateboarding down a hill. I raced down the hill, without any protective gear, as quickly as I could, allowing the hot desert air to slap at my face. When I lost control, I tried to bail, tried to feign running through the air fast enough to hit the ground and keep moving. When I came down, I didn't stand a chance. My hands hit first, and gravity scraped me along the asphalt for several feet before leaving me to rest. My army buddies told me earlier that day it was a dangerous hill to speed down, and I was stupid for trying. Later that week, my boss threatened to charge me with dereliction of duty for skateboarding when I was on-call. (Soldiers have this myth, and I never knew whether or not it was true, that troops engaging in self-destructive behaviors can be charged with damaging government property—themselves.) The doctor cut open both of my hands and tried to bolt the bones back together. When he opened up the left hand, the bone was worse off than he thought, so he slipped in a cadaver donor's scaphoid while I was under for surgery. He told me just as casual as that, the day after, in a recovery bed.

Army doctors get away with a lot.

In a cubicle where I wait for the benefits administrator to come talk to me, there is a pamphlet for *Atomic Veterans*. That's what Veterans Affairs calls vets exposed to ionizing radiation during America's atomic era. It's common enough that they have a name for it. Vets stationed outside of Hiroshima and Nagasaki, but also veterans near testing ranges in the U.S., and vets who were intentionally exposed to radiation for the sake of testing its impact on the human body.

Many vets in these latter categories were sworn to silence, and for decades they couldn't legally discuss their exposure to anyone, including medical professionals. By the time a law came along to allow them to seek the treatment that many of them need, many were already dead. Those still living had been carrying the secret for so long that they still didn't come forward. The pamphlet in front of me is an effort to reach out to those atomic veterans, to let them know that they are legally able to speak up, and to seek treatment for their wounds.

I'm here because I need medical insurance, and because I need to document skateboarding injuries that Veterans Affairs considers "service-related" because I was in the army when they happened.

I don't belong here.

Arms

I collected a history on each arm as I served. At times my choices bent toward tradition: sailors who operated a ship's anchor windlass often tattooed hinges in the 'ditches' of their elbows. Other times, resistance: the posters of radical political cartoonist Mike Flugennock decorate each shoulder. Sometimes pride: the purple, pink, and blue stars reflect the bisexual pride flag. Other times, penance: the pistol and skull on my arm came near my departure from service. With the sense of doom that hung over all of us soldiers, my early twenties saw the addition of a marking that grows more humorous as it ages—"Live fast, die young" tattooed on my biceps.

Soldiers love slogans. Greggs' forearm dagger declared "death before dishonor." Abel's shoulder pistols were wrapped with "Assist, Protect, Defend." Levi's back was a memento mori: "Die Trying." Names and dates of the fallen are common. So too is the Soldier's Creed: *I will never quit.* Something simple. Something meaningful. A saying to rally to, even if it isn't true.

I blame the Roman poet Horace, who gave us the first such lie: *Dulce et decorum est pro patria mori.*

Head

The second decade of the new millennium is filled with tracts on the reintegration of the warrior into non-military culture. What we missed. Who we are. Women and men caught between worlds. Reintegration. Assimilation. Transition.

It's true, of course, but most of this commentary misses the point. It's not just combat or PTSD or war ripping through those closest to you. It's culture shock. The military has its own rules. Its own values. Its own language. One can still be locked up for adultery in the military, or even consensual sodomy. A soldier can lose several months' pay and be confined to her barracks room just for being mouthy to her boss.

When I got out of the military, I took an internship with the biggest LGBT rights organization in the country. Months earlier, I was a staff sergeant, broad-shouldered and in charge of training dogs to detect bombs for missions protecting the President of the United States. A dog and I worked with Secret Service, protecting the world's leaders. We trained with real bombs. Carried real guns. Real cowboy shit.

Then I was an intern. A college student.

I overdressed my first day as an intern, in a tie and slacks and short-cropped hair among T-shirts and skirts. But I stood out in other ways too. I worried about playing streaming music or using social media at my desk. I hesitated to join the early-twenties interns on afternoon food-truck runs. Progressive youth talk with their own code—right and wrong are a language they've honed in their last few years of college, and the gray ethics of military service during Iraq and Afghanistan left me an outsider from the start.

"How old are you?" one college junior asked me with a raised eyebrow in our shared cubicle space. I had to relearn my position, as a young adult, as a worker, as a queer person. New language, new values. I felt, at once, years ahead and years behind my peers. That sort of displacement disorients everything. The veteran examines each action to determine if it makes sense under these new rules. Working at a university now, I find myself questioning every utterance; *does this sentence make sense to civilians, or is my army showing?*

Did you hear the one about the cookies sent to the deployed soldier? About the marine and the professor? The veterans and the school desk? The on-base bar filled with wives the week after deployment?

Veterans have their own mythologies, and the underlying theme of these stories is easy to read: fear of being alone.

Humiliated. Left behind. Forgotten. The war in Afghanistan ended (again) in December of 2014. The story made a blip in the news, but competed with the normalization of relations between the U.S. and Cuba, the shooting of two NYC officers, and reports of hacking at Sony ahead of the release of a particularly belligerent film about North Korea.

Our generation has no V-J Day parade. We serve far from home, and life moves forward without us. We return to find everything changed, and our identities developed differently than those who stayed, and when all fanfare and pride have receded, we often feel embarrassed for having to catch up. We took a different path than our peers, and when we leave that path, we must often backtrack before we can move forward.

We are left with this mark, on our resumes, of course, where we must show that during the period of our lives when we should have been writing for a university newspaper and running for student government, we were walking around with guns strapped to our hips. We have to wear the mark too, carry ourselves knowing that we volunteered during a particularly ugly time, and that no one really cares. Don't get me wrong, Veterans Affairs is stronger than ever and the new GI Bill offers vets a real chance to transform themselves and their lives, but the place left for the veteran in contemporary society is pity, and that is the real badge we wear. Veterans aren't ignorant of the fact that the spirit of "hire a vet" flag-waving isn't a recognition of the personal and professional development we undertook during our service; it is a charity, a service to the community.

Whether we deployed or not, we all left home, those of us who served in the years following The Day the Towers Fell. The world kept moving, and now we must either catch up, or stay lost in the desert.

Heart
On my chest I left a mark, a heart, anatomic in design, with a quote: "Get busy living, or get busy dying." Stephen King. A phrase I found particularly evocative in my youth, con-

necting it to blurred motivations behind why I joined the army and why I chose to leave it.

This isn't about that. Or it is, I suppose, indirectly.

Mental health professionals talk about the moral injury military service leaves on veterans. Emotional conflicts arising from the transgressions of one's moral and ethical beliefs. Vets experience this sort of injury not only from their own actions, but from the acts of "peers and leaders who betray expectations in egregious ways."

Disclaimer: I've never killed anybody.

Disclaimer: Never ask a veteran if they've killed somebody.

Yet in early 2003, as U.S. ground troops moved from Kuwait into Iraq, as people around the world marched together as a plea for peace, I trained as a rooftop gunner, preparing all year with my fingers on the trigger of a machine gun.

Later that year, when the world learned that young military police had humiliated and terrorized detainees in Abu Ghraib prison using dogs, feces, nudity, and threats, I wore an armband embroidered with crossed pistols and "MP," and then ran off to become a dog handler.

I said nothing in 2005, when members of my unit recently returned from the corrections center at Guantanamo Bay laughed and joked about the BBQs and the Quick Reaction Forces that scuffed up detainees at the illegal prison. I said nothing when a young corporal from United States Regional Correctional Facility—Korea giggled as he told me how forced washings started with the ass and crotch before moving to the face. I said nothing when my thrice-deployed colleague told me that he couldn't wait to get back, because "shooting at Haji is simpler than dealing with ex-wife bullshit."

In the months-long ritual that turns citizens into warriors, service members are instilled with a new moral code. When and how it is alright to kill. Why we must follow orders. Who the good guys are, who the bad guys are, and why the world is black and white. This acculturation process is meant to make the act of combat mechanical. Soldier is told, soldier does. Something else happens to the self during this period too: indoctrination beyond "follow orders." It is the formation of *We,* a process in which supporting the in-group rises above doing what is right.

It's violation of this black and white that causes bewilderment. How does one mend the ethics of Haditha when the villains are wearing the same costumes as you? Abu Ghraib? Guantanamo Bay? Ramadi?

The fog of real life has no place in war.

PHOTO: CHILDREN ARDENT FOR SOME DESPERATE GLORY

TUMBLEWEED IS NOT the state flower of Nevada.

Tourists and locals alike mistakenly believe that wandering corpse that litters the Great Basin most of the year is that of sagebrush, the official state flower, *Artemisia tridentata* officially. This is all wrong (tumbleweed is Russian thistle, not sagebrush), but somehow this myth persists. Perhaps it is because one can't help but to look over the shrub-speckled desert that spans most of the Silver State and think of tumbleweed, that American symbol of loneliness and austerity. Perhaps it is because, like tumbleweed, the muted tones of the sagebrush invoke a character of the West: lonely and low, living or dying with a scarcity of resources, far away from the known world.

Though the photo is of the desert, the landscape is not the first thing one notices. At first the eye goes to the seven of us, teenagers with our arms linked over each other's shoulders. We're in T-shirts and faded jeans. Ball caps and a motocross jersey. Being young, queer, and poor, I'm in jelly bracelets and stolen raver pants. We're smiling a smile that doesn't yet recognize that it is doomed, but there is something about the horizon just behind us, rocky outcroppings of a sagebrush-spotted hill, that seems appropriately bleak.

This is one of the last of photos of me before I go, before I use the war machine to escape the desert basin of Reno, Nevada. This is the last photo of me in dyed hair, the last photo of my wispy chinstrap beard. This is the last time that the seven of us will be together in a photo, before the winds carry away those of us who have torn up our roots, before those with roots settle in with jobs they hate or bellies ripe with future workers.

Alexis and her sister Jess stay, and within a few years they are well on their way to a family of barefooted children, a tribe of toddlers who will grow up in the same sort of dirty kitchens as those of us in the photo did. Children who will grow up to lose their virginity on the same sort of hand-me-down couches, who will learn about sex and life on television and through bad decisions as their parents work double shifts and leave them unattended after school. This is history repeating itself, the generational echo of growing up hopeless. What else is there to do in the Biggest Little City but to fuck with futureless abandon between shifts propping up the city's tourist industry? This is how we learn love in the desert.

Mary stayed too, and she doubled-down on being a parent. In contrast to the void we latchkey kids experienced—where we made out and played video games and drank nothing but can after can of caffeinated soft drinks—Mary grew into a super mom. You know the type, the momtivist who champions home-birth, preaches about *intactivism*, breastfeeds even as children start school, shares anti-vaccination posts on social media. Mary built a response to the childhood we came up through, and built an identity around motherhood instead of accepting it as a default status. In the photo she is behind me, with her arm wrapped around me in a way that scares me—I worry that if I would have stayed, I would be the 9-to-5-and-overtime husband whose sole mission is to support a wife and kids. The way she hugs me here conjures up this alternate future where I have a queer second life that sneaks around to meet men on Grindr, the gay men's hookup app, before shifts in the lumberyard, or the casino, or a car lot slinging four-wheel-drives in the desert heat.

My cousin Brian became a parent too, though a bit differently. He isn't a stay-at-home dad to push gender norms or to be an activist. His wife makes money, so he raises kids. You might expect that those of us with bad teeth hold on to some sort of masculine ideal, but the truth is that while we were raising ourselves on a diet of Hot Pockets and ramen noodles, we were also forming our own sense of right and wrong, rejecting both traditional working-class expectations and the popular depictions of family on television to figure it out on our own.

Phil and little Andy fled Reno too, though in quite different directions. After jumping from place to place, job to job, after near brushes with the law, after not knowing which way to go, Phil landed in Alaska, America's last frontier. We don't speak because of the usual reason that men who date women don't speak (a shared romantic interest), but he got away too, ran to anywhere but the bleakness of the high desert. The chubby little redhead in the photo, the smallest of us, swelled to the size of a warrior and joined the ranks of the police. Those who don't come from lack often fail to understand why our men fill the ranks of the military and police forces. It isn't just toxic masculinity. It isn't just being raised by first-person shooter games. It's because being told you can be a hero when there are so few life rafts in sight is a particularly alluring siren's call. When your parents haven't saved enough to fix the car, let alone send you to college, any opportunity seems appealing. When your parents know how to file for SNAP, but don't know what FAFSA stands for, you reach for the safety that is closest. This isn't ignorance, or even desperation; it's just survival.

For the life of me, I cannot remember what it is that we are all smiling about in the photo. We're in the north valleys, where working-class white and brown people cluster in cheap homes and trailer parks, a place none of us have any particular affinity for. Yet I remember that I am *out* as a bisexual in the photo, and that my friends experience this as a non-issue. I know that Andy and Jess are happy to be hanging out with their older sibling. I know that Brian, Phil, and Alexis are either about to have, or already have had, their first threesome together. I know that I have yet to convince Mary that dating someone who is in love with someone else is causing her streak of bad luck.

The light of the picture reveals itself as the burnt gold of late summer, and I know that by this time the following year, all but the youngest of us would be on our own, figuring out our own way after years of practice raising ourselves at home. By this time the following year, we will all have jobs working for entities we don't really believe in. Within a year, I will be on a plane to my first duty station in the U.S. Army, a tiny base in a foreign country, a fifteen-hour flight away from here, far from the desert, far from latchkey homes, grasping at the first life raft that can float me to safety.

WHAT SEPTEMBER LEFT

"ANTHONY WILLIAM MOLL." Not just Tony, but my full name. "I need you to come out here and explain this to me." It wasn't a shout that my mother cast across our house just outside of Reno, but her voice was raised. It wasn't anger, not exactly; her voice held back panic.

The house was always dim. The curtains—where we had them—were always pulled, the venetian blinds always down. In my bedroom, a dark cave in the back of the house, I had hung a thick comforter across the window to block the midday light that woke me most afternoons. Rolling off a futon, I groped through the pile of clothes and books that littered the room and pulled out a pair of jeans I could slide on before following her voice to the dining room.

I knew what this was about. I knew what she had found, what I had left on the dining room table just hours earlier for her to find: official papers listing my social security number, birth date, and the results of my recent physical examination tucked neatly in a folder with a single star and the U.S. Army's current motto, "Army of One," stamped across the front.

"Care to explain this?" she asked, waving the folder at me with one hand before taking a long drag from a cigarette with the other.

"I'm leaving."

She rolled her eyes. "Oh, you're leaving. Did you think at all to ask me about this, or your dad? When are you going to talk to the recruiter? One of us will go down there with you."

"Mom."

"Don't—Don't you dare '*Mom*' me."

"Mom, this has nothing to do with you."

It had everything to do with her. My mother—who spent more time ensuring that rent was paid than she did raising us in the traditional way—didn't teach me much in way of how to live one's life, but she did tell me from the time I could read that I needed to keep my grades up, and I needed to be the first to go to college, and that young men who did not do so were at risk of being drafted or tricked into joining the army. For me to toss that lesson out entirely not only meant rejecting her position, but it made real one of her greatest anxieties.

"Besides, it's already done. I've signed the contract. I'm leaving; I'm getting out of Reno."

"We could have come to the recruiter with you—Christ—you can't join the army with pink hair. Do you even know what the army is like? How do you know he didn't trick you into something that you don't yet know about?" She tossed the folder down on the old oak table and shook her head. "This isn't—you couldn't have just signed everything that quickly."

"Jesus, Mom. I'm not stupid. I didn't get tricked into anything."

I never gave my mother much credit—both because she was frequently a mess, and because I was a teenager—but in that moment, panicked and angry, she was right, and I was wrong, on both counts.

★

"Hello, Is this Mr. Moll?"

As an eighteen-year-old barista with dyed hair and facial piercings, no one called me Mr. Moll.

"Who is this?"

"This is Staff Sergeant Lamonda with U.S. Army Recruiting. Am I speaking with Mr. Moll today?"

"Yeah. Yeah, this is Mr. Moll."

"I'm calling to talk to you about a well-paying career with the United States Army. Can I ask you a question Mr. Moll? What do you do now for a living?"

"I . . . uh . . . I work in a bookstore." This was a half-truth. I worked at a café in a bookstore. I served coffee to book shoppers back when people still bought books in stores.

"Great, and do you like it? If you don't mind me asking, how much does that pay?"

"Not enough."

"I bet. We hear a lot of that. Listen, our office spoke with you about a year ago, and you said then that you weren't really interested in sitting down with us. If that's still the case, that's fine, of course, but I was wondering if anything had changed in your life, and if so, if you'd be interested in coming in and chatting. No commitment, just talking with us about what you want, about what sort of career you're looking for."

Of course things had changed in my life. Everything had changed in my life. I had gone from one odd teenage job to another: pizza shop, bookstore café, even the kid who fixed the arcade machines at Chuck E. Cheese. I had broken up, then gotten back together, then broken up, then gotten back together with a girl from a nice neighborhood. I had recognized the hopelessness of my situation, stuck in the valleys north of town where working-class folks held warehouse jobs and started accidental families younger than they should. I kept saying that I would soon head to college, community college to start, but the truth is, I didn't know how to apply to college, and neither did my parents, who went straight to work after high school. I didn't know how grants worked, or even loans, or even where to start. Teachers told me throughout my teens that I was bright, but everyone knew that I wouldn't be the first bright stone to be lost in Nevada's foothills.

Then there were the planes. In retrospect, part of me hates to admit that it was the planes—too cliché, too predictable, too perfectly responsive to the narrative the nation crafted in the wake of it all. But just months earlier, on a boring September morning, a few hours before my boring shift at a boring job, I found myself half-dressed and staring at my television, slack-jawed with awe, floating in helplessness. Looking back later, we will all know that this is how they got us: that feeling of vulnerability. It's how a selfish nation rallied ourselves into enlisting, to donating blood, to volunteering time, to hanging a flag up on the porch. *Surely, we don't live in a world where buildings can be felled by planes, where shining cities can be transmuted into smoke plumes. Surely, there is something we can do.* And so, all across the country in the months that followed that morning, the idle hands of people who felt helpless were turned into the hands of volunteers, police, firefighters, and, of course, soldiers.

"Yeah. I might come chat with you. When can I come in?"

"Two weeks?" my mother gasped. "That's not enough time to uproot your whole life. What about your job? What about packing? What if your dad and I go down there and talk to him, straighten this all out?"

"There's nothing to straighten out. This is a new job, a better job. Besides, I'd rather go now than wait around and have people try to talk me out of it."

"What are you going do? You're going to drive tanks? You're going to be a medic?"

"The military police."

"What are you talking about? You don't even like the police!"

She was mostly right, but I would never let her know it. For many who grew up poor, the police didn't seem like a group of people around to help us. For us, police were the men with the guns. Police were the ones who caused us trouble. They were the ones who chased dirtbag kids like us when we skateboarded through mall parking lots, the ones who assumed we had drugs on us when they caught us. Police wanted me in juvenile hall. Police oversaw our road-side work-crew of teenage delinquents. Our fathers and our siblings were afraid of the police. Our communities avoided calling the police. The military police were a default choice for me. I scored excellently on the test given to prospective recruits, but I was also eager and desperate to leave home in a hurry. When I was told I couldn't be placed in any of my first three jobs within the next couple of months, I took the next thing they offered me, personal ethics be damned.

Her long, chipped nails tapped against the table as she talked to me. She alternated quick drags from her cigarette and sips from her soda can as she tried to figure a way out of this.

"Where will you go?"

"Seventeen weeks in Missouri."

"Then?"

I shrugged. "Could be anywhere after that."

"I just—I don't get why you would do this, Tony. Boys like you don't just go and join the army. What about college? What about the war?"

Again, she was right. I was the sort of boy who played video games, who went to raves and punk shows and flirted with boys. I was not the kind of person who joined the army. Except that I was poor, which made me exactly the type of person who joined the army. That made college a factor I had considered; like many of the enlisted men and women of my time, college was the carrot that lured us in.

Money for college offered the promise of the army as a stepladder. At some ambiguous point in the future, I'd be a college-educated man, not a tent-sleeping grunt, and certainly not a midday-waking barista still living with his parents in a rat trap of a desert town. War was another factor I had considered—though on that point, I had significantly miscalculated.

"They've been bombing since October. How long do you really think the war will last? By the time I'm done in June, we'll probably be all wrapped up."

HEADLINES FROM THE *RENO GAZETTE-JOURNAL* THE MORNING OF SEPTEMBER 11, 2001

CENSUS FIGURES Show a Gender Gap in the Silver State, Comeback? Jordan Almost Certain to Return, Fear Grows as Well Runs Low, Payroll Tax Cut Sought, Warnings Preceded California Rampage, Ex-Death Row Inmate Accused of 2nd '78 Killing, Court Blocks FAA From Limited Pilots' Work Hours, GOP Law Makers Want Action, NATO Destroys Arms From Rebels, Bush Promotes Education Package, Iraq Says Airstrike Killed 8 Civilians, GOP Reassures Social Security Recipients, Parents Press to See Jailed Aid Workers, Grand Jury Rejects Complaint Against Condit, Suspected Cow Disease Discovered in Japan, Butte Residents Go Home—Fire Continues, Nevada Water Dispute Focuses on Rural County, Residents Benefit from Ward Offices, Survival of What We Deem the Fittest, WNCC's Generous Benefactor Give Students More Choices, Last Chance to Have Your Say, 70% to 95% of Victims Survive Lightning Strikes, Pack Backs Rewarded for Rushing Efforts, He's Looking More Like Custer, Bullnanza Reno May Have Venue Change for 2002, NHL Accused of Importing Too Many Europeans, Child Sex Suspect Wants Confession Videos Suppressed, Ace Pilot Overcomes Mishaps and Bad Attitude, Firm Seeks

Railroad Trench Contract, Postal Worker to Make Bid for Reno Mayor, Workers Seek New Law for Casual-Labor Site, Accident Victim Lived Life in the Fast Lane, Police Standoff Ends Quietly, Judge Clears Carson City Deputy DA, Environmental Groups Protest Logging, Big Unlimited Class Planes Warm Up for Races, Ag Boss Apprehensive About Medical Marijuana, Washoe Schools Plan to Hire Retired Educators, Volunteer Mounted Patrols Try to Control Wild Horses, Slot Player Loses Battle Over Disputed Jackpot, Light Snow but Higher Earnings for Resorts, Production of Gold Up Despite Higher Prices, Gizmo Telecommunications Moves to Reno—Stores to Follow, American Skiing to Sell Sugarbush, GE Chief Says He Was Too Cautious, Latin Grammys Get Back to Music, Next Skywalker Feels the Force of Instant Fame, With One Twin Gone the Survivor Studies His Loss, Booze as Health Tonic Doesn't Go Down Easily, e-Therapy: Mental Health or Mental Meddling?, How Good Are Buns/Thigh Machines, Book Helps Break Barriers, Gadgets Can Help Even Watchful Parents, Kids—Wash Your Hands!, The Times They're Not a'Changin'.

WRONG AS TWO BOYS, PT. I

THE FIRST real shock was the cattle cars. They sat lined up in a row, boxy trailers sputtering like old pickups, waiting to take the newest recruits of Alpha Company to the barracks on the training side of a military installation in frozen, nowhere Missouri. Our drill sergeants, uniformly red-faced men and women with impractical hats and exploding voices, roared as we were rushed, 30 or 40 of us in a file, into those cans on wheels. Little light made its way into the trailer as we pushed together closer than many of us had ever stood next to a stranger: close enough that we could feel not only the breath of the person behind us, but the rise and fall of his or her chest. We would learn during the upcoming weeks to refer to this loading method with the same eloquent language as our drill sergeants: *nuts to butts.*

Packed in, we listened to the monsters outside scream at the remaining recruits to squeeze in, until we heard the doors smash shut and we felt our first lurch. The convoy began to move. As our truck jerked forward, the heap of us fell back, yet being so tightly pressed together, we stayed on our feet, instead only feeling the weight of those around us as we all lost our balance. I didn't know then that the windows were covered during the trip to leave us feeling disoriented, but I should have. In the dark interior of the trailer, as we rumbled over the unfamiliar roads to the place we'd live together for the next seventeen weeks, none of us made a sound.

When I joined in early 2002, the only references I had for army life were *M*A*S*H** and *G. I. Joe.* I didn't have a big brother who had served, nor a parent. I didn't grow up near a base. None of my friends from high school had rushed off to join. Until a recruiter called me up, I didn't even know that soldiers were paid a salary.

So it surprised everyone, myself included, when—as an overdramatic, eighteen-year-old queer kid with spikey, dyed hair—I enlisted, signing up to be whisked off less than three weeks after the first call from the recruiting office. Few of us had a superhero-like origin story for why we joined. Mine was a muddled recipe: uneven parts teenage wanderlust, the emotional gut-punch from the attacks in New York and D.C. just months earlier, and a desire to escape from my stagnant situation in a working-class home by any means necessary. Reno—and dusty, dying cities like it all over the country—export a great many of its youth to the military.

On the trucks rumbling through Fort Leonard Wood, I no longer wore pink hair. It was buzzed down as short as the hack of a barber could slice it in the minute or so he had for each recruit. Like the dozens of other young men packed into the box with me, I wore only brown peach-fuzz on my scalp, and like everyone else I saw, my anxious eyes seemed to silently ask what came next.

When the cattle trucks came to a stop, ours was not the first to unload. We stood nervously, sweating all over each other, as the indecipherable shouts of the drill sergeants boomed through the winter air outside. The minutes stretched out as we waited, until the doors of our truck cracked open, allowing the light to leak, and then flood, the interior. With no further warning, we spilled out in two files, rushing out of the truck like an unplugged faucet. When my turn came, I took a small jump from the final step of the trailer onto the hard Missourian dirt. One foot planted squarely, and before the other could do the same, my attempt to put the duffel bag I had been carrying onto my back failed, tipping my balance, swinging me to the ground. I remember two impacts. The first: my body hitting the dirt. The second: the ferocity of a swarm of drill sergeants descending upon me, their fallen prey.

The shouts came from everywhere.

"GETTHEFUCKUP!"

"Move, Private, Move!"

"On your feet! Now! Now! Now!"

Memory is an odd-shaped tool. Though I hazily recall the fall and the shouts, the moment that really stuck happened next. As I came to my feet and the frenzy of drill sergeants moved on to the next recruit out of the truck, one particular drill sergeant—one with a bright red face and enormous veins—leaned in and, instead of yelling, spoke quietly into my ear.

"Private, there's that one guy in every cycle, the fuck-up who nobody wants on their side. Are you going to be *that guy?*"

No one wants to be that guy, but particularly not a queer kid serving in an army that harasses and discards (or worse) men and women who aren't heterosexual. I spent the next several months doing everything I could not to be that guy. The military made the following eight years of my life an exercise in blending in.

Ask an older vet and they'll tell you the army is nothing like it was back when they went through. Back when the drill sergeants were allowed to swear. Back when they could hit you. Desert Storm, Kosovo, Vietnam. Old Army.

When I went through, we were told, during in-processing, that the drill sergeants were not allowed to swear anymore.

Like so much in our government, this is only really true on paper. They swore, of course, but they also tried their best to mind their language while tearing into us. Most of them attempted their fury while shouting out things like "Jiminy flippin' Cricket, Private." We learned quickly not to chuckle at these attempts. Yet not all the drill sergeants would submit to that sort of censorship. Drill Sergeant Michaels had no reservations about swearing, nor about letting us know the when and how of lectures from his senior officer any time a private would complain—through anonymous channels—about his swearing.

"Jesus Christ, Privates," said Michaels before us one night as the whole company of recruits strained in the up position of a push-up with the sun setting behind us. "One of you shitheads ran your mouth again about my language offending your tender little ears. I try to be genuine with you fuckers and this is how you repay me. That's wrong, Privates. That's wrong as two boys fucking."

When I took the oath of enlistment in February of 2002, just weeks earlier, I naively misjudged the reality of the policy called "Don't Ask, Don't Tell." An hour or so before our oath, toward the end of the process, a uniformed man handed each recruit a memo that included the exact language of the policy, spelled out in precise legalese:

A member of the armed forces shall be separated from the armed forces under regulations prescribed by the Secretary of Defense if one or more of the following findings is made and approved in accordance with procedures set forth in such regulations:

1. *That the member has engaged in, attempted to engage in, or solicited another to engage in a homosexual act or acts unless there are further findings, made and approved in accordance with procedures set forth in such regulations, that the member has demonstrated that—*

A. *such conduct is a departure from the member's usual and customary behavior;*

B. *such conduct, under all the circumstances, is unlikely to recur;*

C. *such conduct was not accomplished by use of force, coercion, or intimidation;*

D. *under the particular circumstances of the case, the member's continued presence in the armed forces is consistent with the interests of the armed forces in proper discipline, good order, and morale; and*

E. *the member does not have a propensity or intent to engage in homosexual acts.*

2. *That the member has stated that he or she is a homosexual or bisexual, or words to that effect, unless there is a further finding, made and approved in accordance with procedures set forth in the regulations, that the member has demonstrated that he or she is not a person who engages in, attempts to engage in, has a propensity to engage in, or intends to engage in homosexual acts.*

3. *That the member has married or attempted to marry a person known to be of the same biological sex.*

Got it. It seemed simple enough. Don't get caught having gay sex, don't say that I'm gay, and don't marry a man. Simple. Though I wasn't very far into basic training when I grasped how this policy played out as rampant homophobia, fueled by an expectation that everyone within earshot at any given time was heterosexual. "Wrong as two boys fucking" wouldn't go away after basic training; it would get worse. This phrase wasn't an isolated utterance. It was a common adage all over the military, among so many whom I served with. The first time stung. Just stung, yet the cumulative weight of this silly expression and what it meant—for me, for the culture I had just forced upon myself by enlisting, the culture in which I found myself an emotionally isolated young man 1,500 miles from home—felt enormous.

★

Standing in full gear on the bayonet training range, I would be ignorant to the fact that naivety is what feeds the U.S. military. When I left home, I was just as unprepared for the language of violence that I found in basic training as I was for the homophobia. Why? Youth. Working-class nationalism. The human desire to believe in something wholly. As a kid who rebelled left against parents who swung right, I fled home wanting to believe in a mature and responsible military that adhered to international laws on humane treatment of its opponents, the military of a *City on a Hill*.

This violence played out everywhere in basic training, but most obviously on the bayonet training range. I guess that it should have surprised me most that, in the 21st century, the army still trains soldiers to fight with bayonets. What stunned me though came in the chants we were guided through to motivate us during this training. In a giant field of packed dirt with evenly spaced scarecrow-like figures standing every ten meters or so, we moved in helmets and armored vests with our rifles in hand, bayonets affixed. A drill sergeant stood on a raised wooden platform, calling out commands. Stab. Buttstroke. Rifle Push. With all of our intensity, we would strike at the heavy wooden and rubber figures before us in unison. The other drill sergeants would wander about the field, ensuring that we were putting everything we had into each blow. They even had us screaming with every strike, just shouting, as loud as we could, as we assaulted the scarecrow. In an attempt to keep us motivated, the elevated drill sergeant would occasionally shout out calls to which we were expected to reply with absurdly violent responses.

"What is the spirit of the rifle bayonet fighter?"

Chorus: "To kill, kill, kill without mercy!"

"What are the two types of soldiers?" he shouted through a bullhorn.

Chorus: "The quick and the dead!"

One Sunday in early May, we sat scattered along the concrete slab that lay in front of our brick barracks, shining our boots with wax and spit. At that point, twelve or so weeks into basic training, that was our idea of a relaxing Sunday afternoon. The Missourian heat and humidity didn't feel unreasonable just yet, and we had all started to loosen up a bit with each other. Those laid-back days were among the few moments we had to relax during the process.

"Watch it, faggot!"

The statement rang out behind me like an alarm. Behind us, one bull-headed recruit snapped at the man who accidentally kicked the boot wax he had been using. "Why don't you watch where you're going?"

Faggot stung. More than stung. Lee, the angry instigator, didn't mean to imply that the soldier had sex with other men; he meant to insult him by calling him a sissy, a feminine man who didn't belong in the army. He wielded the *faggot* that I had grown up with: the faggot who isn't interested in sports, the faggot who complains to teachers and parents, the faggot who dyes his hair.

Faggot shifted something in me, something like a newly found sense of American masculinity (in the worst way). Something like nerd rage, queer rage.

"You southern piece of shit," I snapped back. "Don't let me catch you using that word again."

Lee and I both jumped to our feet, and the exchange that followed was what many would expect. It involved the colorful language of soldiers. It involved intense eye contact. Chest-to-chest contact. Performative masculinity. It involved one or more friends interrupting with an "it's not worth it, man." Growing up on the wrong end of bullying gives one a distaste for conflict: a high school manifestation of fight or flight. My body shook with that sense for flight. My body agreed, this was not worth it, yet I also ached with a fresh sense to fight. My boot brush quivered in my clenched fist. My face glowed red. The reaction was unfamiliar to me, and my body wasn't sure how to handle it. The stare-down finished as these things often do, our buddies calmed us down, and the matter was dropped, and we all started back on our boots. We left the interaction hanging in the air.

"Are you okay, man?" another soldier seated beside me asked, noticing my reaction.

"I'm fine," I lied, barely holding in angry tears. "He's just a fuckin' asshole."

An hour or so later, I was the first of our platoon to trickle back into the barracks when Personal Time (boot shining and letter writing) ticked into Hygiene Time. I headed to the bathroom, a cleaned-twice-a-day, group-style latrine, where the rows of sinks still sparkled and smelled of cleaner from this morning's scrub down. I stood in front of one of the mirrors, attempting to rinse my face and regain my cool, still a little shaken.

Lee arrived next. When the bathroom door swung open, it was obvious that he was looking for someone.

"You wanna run your mouth now that the drill sergeants aren't around?"

"Lee, you aren't going to fight me in the barracks," I told him without breaking my gaze into the mirror. "You know we'd both get in trouble." Good job. Play it cool. Nonchalance. Indifference. Cool.

"You think I give a shit?" he shouted back, smacking his hand on the wall near the mirror. His voice grew increasingly louder. Because I knew that mine would get shaky and pubescent if I did the same, I feigned calmness.

The bathroom where we stood was positioned between the shower room and the changing room. Getting undressed in the barracks would take place exclusively in this changing room. When we bathed, each of us would walk through the bathroom in flip-flops and with a coarse, brown towel wrapped around our waist in order to get to the shower room. The rest of our platoon had been filing into the barracks right behind him as he entered, and our peers had begun the rush to the changing room and were by now in various states of undress. Lee's voice caught the attention of those nearby, including a buddy of mine, Ackerman, who popped his head around the corner from the changing room.

"You're not going to fight him," he told Lee calmly.

"Mind your own business, Ackerman."

The barracks roommate standing up for me was the sort of guy I had avoided my whole life. Southern. Jockish. Confrontational. He rushed toward action, instead of shrinking from it. He believed in a traditional sense of right and wrong.

Swinging around the corner in his towel and flip-flops, Ackerman pushed his stocky chest out and furrowed his brow as he approached. He thrust his bare chest into Lee.

Ackerman did not share my desire to avoid conflict in the barracks. Lee too seemed indifferent to the potential consequences that a fight might bring. The two reenacted the pose I had tried on earlier: one man's chest pressed to another's. Eye contact. Flared nostrils.

Like any good school-yard melee, there were varying accounts of who hit first.

All any of us saw were the two bodies, one towel-clad and the other still in army shorts and T-shirt, colliding. A punch or two were whipped through the air, and the scuffle quickly made its way to the floor.

"FIGHT!" someone shouted into the hall outside as both a promotion and a warning.

Men swarmed into the bathroom. Dressed men from the halls. Half-dressed men from the changing room. Naked men from the shower room. Those close to me and Ackerman rushed to pull Lee off of him. Lee's buddies attempted the same to Ackerman. Those most concerned with the punishment for fighting in the barracks rushed over in an effort to stop the whole thing. Each addition to the clash caused only more chaos. People were tackled to the polished floor. More punches were thrown, more shouting, and through it all, little concern was paid to nudity. Dicks and asses tumbled throughout the bathroom. Exposed men bear-hugged other men while others formed a dog pile atop the cold blue tiles. Hairy body parts were flung through the air haphazardly.

It was the gayest thing I had ever seen.

I remained untouched by the scuffle. When it broke out, I stood there by the sink, mouth open, my face clearly express-ing shock at the tangle of human limbs and hair that had formed. The jumble eventually resolved organically; at some point, everyone just got up off of each other, calmed their heavy breathing and headed back to get their shower, luck-ily before the drill sergeants had heard a thing. Without much ado, everyone dusted off their clothes, or nude thighs and shoulders in some cases, and got back to life. Pressure released. All systems returned to normal. Afterward, Acker-man approached me with a gruff but content look on his face.

"Christ, man. Thanks," I told him, still stunned by the whole affair.

He nodded, confident he had, in some sort of way, won. "No sweat, brother."

A few hours later, Els—a handsome solider with terra-cotta skin who dwelled in the mind of half of the women in our training unit—slipped next to me as I brushed my teeth at the same sink where the mess had begun a couple hours earlier.

"That was really brave of you, standing up like that," he said, pulling out his toothbrush and keeping his glance toward his own mirror.

"Thanks. I wasn't actually involved in the fight; it was stupid—just something I had said earlier."

"That's what I meant, speaking up like that. It was brave."

I found myself suddenly trying to process what I thought was a more basic conversation. *What is going on here?*

I glanced into the mirror and toward his face. His lips formed a small smile and his eyes met mine.

Wait. Is this flirting?

"Thanks." I quickly rinsed off my toothbrush, collected my hygiene bag and started toward my bunk. Flirting was a skill that I considered myself at least competent in, but I had been caught off guard. It only added to my anxiety that this handsome guy was possibly coming on to me in our basic training barracks, where so much as a sideways glance at someone of the same sex could cause a scuffle like the one earlier that night. I didn't want to imagine what would happen to us if someone caught us flirting with a person of the same sex.

Wait, was it flirting? I couldn't be sure. Maybe he was just a stand-up sort of guy.

My answer came, two nights later, in the form of a note, folded tightly and tucked under the pillow of my bunk. I knew who it was from immediately, yet my first thought wasn't about the chance to flirt; it was what could have happened if a drill sergeant had found a note under my pillow. I could barely breathe.

"I'm on fire guard tonight from 1–2. Meet me by the dryers."

He *was* flirting with me.

I tucked the note into my shorts and climbed into my bunk. I set the alarm on my watch for 1 a.m., but I didn't need it. I didn't sleep a bit. I kept thinking about the risks: the risk to meet him, the risk to write the note, the risk of him even approaching me at the sink. I also thought about the fact that I hadn't had sex in over twelve weeks.

I made the only decision I could. I met him, of course, pretending to brush my teeth again, at 1 a.m., in front of the very last sink, the one in front of the dryers.

The bathroom door swung open.

He strutted across the bathroom and sat atop the dryer next to me. I continued the act of pretending to brush my teeth. He watched me for a second, and then spoke softly.

"So, you like guys, right?"

I swallowed a bit of the toothpaste. Still conscious of the risk and not entirely convinced that this wasn't an elaborate trap, I remained cautious. "I don't *not* like guys," I replied, coughing and wiping my face.

"Thought so," he asked as he shifted toward me. His hands moved downward as he stepped toward me, his fingers slipping behind my waistband and around my cock. "What do you think about heading to the shower room?"

This was not a trap. I reacted as quickly as I could, stuttering my way through letting him know I felt both interested and terrified. "I d-d-don't know, I mean, anyone could stumble by us in the shower room, right?"

"Somewhere else then? The room in the back?"

Even as nervous as I felt, I was easy prey. It didn't take much for my fear of getting caught to give way to teenage needs. I nodded and did my best not to appear terrified.

"Let's go," he said in his best attempt at a collected, sexy voice.

His partner on fire guard watched the desk where they were supposed to be stationed for their hour. He told his partner that he needed to write a letter home. I never found out if he knew what we planned to do, but let it be known that his bravery and selflessness were appreciated either way.

The two of us slipped into the back room, a 10"x 10"space with a cold linoleum floor where we had stored all our civilian bags when we moved in. No one ever came in there, and we were well concealed with all the lights off. Still, as we began to make out, my heart was beating out of my chest as my mind wrapped around the possibility of us getting caught.

"What if a drill sergeant walks in?" I whispered.

"Then we're fucked," he said earnestly, his hands slipping back into my shorts.

Not spoken by either of us was what may have happened if one of our comrades would have found us.

I nodded toward the closet in the back corner of the room, and suggested that it might be safer. He agreed, so we stumbled our way through the dark room and into the pitch black, but slightly safer, closet. In the darkness we remained almost entirely silent as we figured everything out by touch. Eager hands. Newly firm waists and hips. Coarse army T-shirts pulled up only halfway.

Of all the surprises during basic training, the one I least predicted was sex in the middle of the night, with a man, inside of military barracks. It was good too, great actually, hot enough to recall years later with some detail. Hot enough to make me blush for weeks when we saw each other at the day's first formation each morning.

Our rendezvous was not my first time, but it *was* my first with a man.

My first time with a man was in the closet.

Later, much later, after the glow wore off, the irony of this situation would be impossible to miss, but the same could be said of its sadness. The eight years that followed involved much more hiding. They involved lying, and sneaking, and all sorts of dishonesty opposing everything the military's rhetoric instills in young troops. Honor. Respect. Courage. The next eight years were an exercise in discovering that "Don't Ask, Don't Tell" meant serving in the army that said I couldn't say or be who I was. I would see more men, in dark rooms, while whispering, but I would never gain the courage to date one, not while in the army. This was a much greater closet. If there was a positive outcome, one beyond quick, hot sex with a beautiful soldier, it was that I always thought of that closet, of masculine lips and strong hands in the dark, every time I heard some leathery, old sergeant tell me something was "wrong as two boys fucking."

MUSCLE MEMORY

"GET YOUR damn face on that rifle, Private."

It must have been early March in Missouri, still gray and cold that year. It had snowed just days prior, and the drill sergeants would only allow us to lay on our stomachs in the prone firing position for fifteen minutes at a time. They were worried about cold-weather injuries, though the damp gravel we were firing from stuck to our uniforms and load-bearing vests even when we stood back up, keeping the cold pinned to us.

The drill sergeant's orders came from behind me as I laid atop the berm that overlooked the once-lush firing range defoliated by late-winter freezes. I didn't want to put my face against the plastic buttstock of the M16 rifle; I was too frightened to put my nose against the aluminum alloy charging handle placed just behind the weapons sights. The moment was my first time behind any sort of weapon, the first time my hands wrapped around the handle and hand-guards of a device meant to ignite and propel a round down-range. My hands shook. They sweated, and the wet eggs and untoasted white bread in my stomach rolled.

During "white phase," the period of basic training in which we began our marksmanship preparation, the drill sergeants had ceased the yelling that had been a nearly round-the-clock chorus since we arrived two and a half weeks earlier. While we had rifles in our hands, while we had a magazine full of 5.56mm, spritzer-shaped rounds, our drill sergeants did not shout. There is an old adage that basic training breaks a person down so that one can be built back up as a warrior. The weeks prior we had been broken down—we felt every shout, and insult, and threat. We felt isolation and fear. We experienced a radical change in sleep, in diet, in notions of personal space. We watched "shark attacks," the coordinated efforts of several drill sergeants simultaneously shouting inches from a recruit's face, spit and sweat slapping against the skin from all directions. Then, the moment we were given rifles, that aggression paused. Though this transition is meant as the first step of the "building up" portion of training, there is also, of course, a very practical reason why one does not shout at emotionally altered young men and women with loaded guns.

So the order to get my damn face on the rifle came as a stern directive, not as a scream.

My fear, one that is not uncommon among those firing weapons for the first time, was that the rifle's recoil, the energy transferred from the explosion inside of the weapon to the firer, would be powerful enough to fuck me up if the weapon slapped my face. In the days prior to the range, we learned about the things that could go wrong when firing, such as what would happen if one of us attempted to fire a round while another round was stuck in the weapon's upper receiver. When we were told that there would be an explosion, my mind wandered to all the things that could mean. What size explosion? What shape? Would the gun swell, like when Bugs Bunny stuck his finger in Elmer Fudd's rifle? Would it just burn my face, or would it ignite my whole body? This was irrational, I know, but so is teaching a nineteen-year-old kid the best ways to knock down targets shaped like human silhouettes.

"Yes, Drill Sergeant," I called back, without looking. The last time someone looked back at one of the drill sergeants instructing us from behind our positions, he turned his rifle with him, turning the loaded muzzle from the targets to everyone—the drill sergeants, the next wave of firers, the cadre who ran the pop-up targets—behind the firing positions. That firer was tackled by a storm of several drill sergeants, and removed from the range rapidly.

I shifted upward, closer to the rifle. As instructed, I ensured that the rifle was tucked tightly to my body: "a single unit." As instructed, I considered how my body was positioned behind the rifle: "an uninterrupted line, extended from the target to the muzzle, down the sights to the buttstock, from the rifle to the shoulder, straight down to your boots." As instructed, I monitored my breathing: "inhale and exhale naturally, firing during the natural respiratory pause at the bottom of the exhale."

An overhead speaker blared over the range. "Left side, clear. Right side, clear. The range is now clear, fire when ready."

As instructed, I squeezed, not pulled, the trigger.

We repeated this process all day, then all week. We were given an acronym—STAB: steady position, trigger squeeze, aim, and breathing. We practiced all day on the range, then we practiced with dummy rifles when we got back to the barracks. Because most of the men and women surrounding me came from a generation raised with video games, the drill sergeants even brought in a Super Nintendo with a modified M16 as a controller. The goal, we were told, is that we repeat the complex process to the point where it feels reflexive. We were internalizing the process, making it mechanical—see a target, fire on a target. We were told this is called muscle memory. For the corn-fed boys and girls, the recruits who grew up with hunting and with shotguns, white phrase was a breeze. A love of shooting was one reason they joined.

For queer boys who spent their high school afternoons rotating punk and dance pop CDs, who spent entire weekends locked in their bedroom painting their nails and playing Resident Evil, STAB and a Super Nintendo are useful educational tools.

The M16 (and the M16 converted to a light gun for the Super Nintendo) is nothing like the Super Scope, a bazooka-style light-gun used for shooting games on that console. It is nothing like the Konami Justifier, a pistol-shaped light-gun designed to replicate the phallic masculinity of a Colt Python. It is not like the Sega Menacer, and the M16 is nothing like the Zapper, the original NES light-gun, the one we used to press to the TV screen as we cheated at *Duck Hunt*. It follows too that firing the M16 does not resemble firing a light-gun. Sure, maybe the timed targets of the range reproduce some of that *Duck Hunt* anxiety, but the army is not a video game.

Right?

Lieutenant Colonel Dave Grossman has written extensively—in his two books regarding the science of killing, *On Killing* and *On Combat*—about the topic of making soldiers mechanical. Among the treatises on teaching men to kill, this author (who remains divisive among those who know him) notes that the U.S. military shifted its training of young men, and later women, after World War II. During the second "war to end all wars," the military found that only 15–20% of infantry troops would actually pull the trigger in a combat situation. For the purposes of military science, these men are called *nonfirers*. The military found that the percentage of nonfirers was reduced by shifting the target shape on which the soldiers trained from stationary circular targets to man-shaped targets that fell when they were hit. The results of such a switch was an increase to 55% of trigger pullers by the time we fought a proxy war in Korea, and 95% by the time we were caught in the snare of Vietnam.

Grossman said, "Psychologists know that this kind of powerful 'operant conditioning' is the only technique which will reliably influence the primitive midbrain processing of a frightened human being."

Drill Sergeant said, "Fire, Private. Knock those Ivans down."

Private Moll said, "Yes, Drill Sergeant."

Ivan. That's what we called our green, spring-loaded opponents on the firing range of Fort Leonard Wood in 2002. Our great red menace, Ivan. Ivan who terrified the Baby Boomers. Ivan who the history books claim was brought down by Reagan and Ronald McDonald. Ivan pops up. Soldier squeezes, not pulls, the trigger. Ivan is defeated.

Much later, when I went on to serve in Korea—where we are told that the Democratic People's Republic of Korea has the capacity to hurl 500,000 rounds of artillery at us within an hour—my squad leader encouraged us to call our targets Kim.

It should be no surprise to anyone that by the time I left the military in 2010, almost a decade into our wars in Iraq and Afghanistan, many service members were calling the targets Haji, the honorific given to Muslims who have completed a pilgrimage to Mecca, and a pejorative some soldiers have given most brown people on the Arabian Peninsula.

At the range, in early March, I think of none of this. I am the machine they want me to be. Though I am new to the weapon, new to the culture, new to the process by which soldiers are indoctrinated, my primary thought is getting my damn face on the rifle. My mind is on S—steady position, T—trigger pull, A—aim, B—breathing. My mind is on Ivan up, squeeze, Ivan down. My mind is on my cheek pressed to the buttstock, my nose touching the charging handle, the green of Ivan appearing on the winter-gray landscape. There is no war. There is nothing outside of this range. No America. No September 11th. No Afghanistan. No Private Moll. It's rather like a video game. The firer himself is gone, off-screen somewhere, and all that matters is mechanical performance. One doesn't have time to consider the dinner plans of the human-shaped pixels we mow down fighting the Red

Falcon Organization. We don't care if the sentries that 007 shoots outside of the Russian dam are just some punk teen-agers who joined the army to pay for college. Not us. That's the stuff of nonfirers. We just STAB. We just shoot.

GREAT BASIN

I don't know why I left
But I know that I done wrong
And it won't be long
'Til I get on back home

MY BRAND NEW body stretches toward the hills. This valley on the western edge of the Great Basin isn't home, not anymore.

It has been only two days since I've been back in Reno, a town primarily known for not being Las Vegas, and I'm already aching to leave. Here in the valley, where the landscape is all pale shrub and stone from my front door until the desert reaches the Sierras in the distance, I'm trying to figure out why I came back in the first place. A matted Chow barks at every car that passes the fence of this dirt and crabgrass yard. Pickup trucks rest in the driveway, and the driveway across the street, and the driveways down the street. A few years ago, my whole family found themselves marooned here in the Biggest Little City and decided to start calling it home.

The army offered me about a week's worth of leave before reporting to my first duty station, a small base 5,600 miles away in South Korea. A few lonely soldiers traveled directly to their new lives, but most of us jumped at the chance to go home and show off how much we had changed. That week was nearing its end, so I decided to do my showing off as I said goodbye.

> Hi Ho Diddly Bop
> I wish I was back on the block
> with that bottle in my hand
> I wanna be a drinking man

I shouldn't drink. I know this. Not just because I'm nineteen, and fresh from seventeen weeks of working out and eating healthy, and down twenty pounds since I left, but because my family has a history of addiction. And bad choices. My father still smokes something that keeps him up and anxious all night. My older brother has transitioned from breaking into cars to selling drugs. My mother can still sit in front one of the hundreds of thousands of video poker machines in this city for hours at a time, more days than not in a given week.

But tonight is a time for celebration, and celebrations are times for regrets. I clink bottles of too-sweet malt booze with Viggy, another newly minted brother-in-arms who followed me home when he didn't have a rat's nest of a family of his own to return to. On our last night in town before running off to be soldiers, we celebrate our brief return and looming departure. We crowd into a house on the edge of town, a valley north of the city that people are embarrassed to say that they are from.

The night is blurry. Annie, the girl who waited for me through basic training, promised her father that nothing unsavory would happen that night, so she goes home before the evening begins its slide. Because she leaves, I stumble into bed with the pudgy and unreserved Alexis loudly enough for everyone to hear as bottles pile up in the crowded kitchen. In the next room, Viggy and a cousin of mine watch and drink as Pearl, the first girl I ever kissed, sleeps with Tabby, the first woman I ever locked bodies with. Then a switch, then another, then regrets, then hiccoughed conversations about the Illuminati on the back porch, where the Sierra foothills begin their climb toward the seamless Tahoe sky, before eventually descending into fog-drenched Sonoma wine country, until the land gives way to the endless Pacific, across which we will travel tomorrow, fresh-cut soldiers who don't know a thing about a damn thing on their way to a new home in the Land of the Morning Calm.

It will remain difficult to untangle this scene. The night is about tongues and limbs and teenage hormones, of course, but it is also about some strange sort of ritual, one that lands somewhere between a sendoff for the doomed, a send up for those who made it out, and a reverence for some role that *home* believes I have become.

> *Your mother was home when you left *you're right!*
> *Your father was home when you left *you're right!*
> *Your brother was home when you left *you're right!*
> *And that's the reason you left *you're right!*

When Pearl, Alexis, Tabby, and my cousin wake up later in the day, they will begin the first of many uncomfortable conversations that begin to repair a night of ignoring all the rules.

Here at dawn though, their bodies are still strewn about a house turned over by celebration, while Viggy and I are concerned only with packing our duffle bags into the back of a car. Though our bodies throb a reminder of the night before, we are able to simply walk away from the fallout unscathed.

As we wrap up and Viggy squeezes close the car doors, I pantomime some final, hungover goodbyes before piling into the car and rolling toward the airport. As morning gold fills the car, and sagebrush and the now-dimmed neon lights of the city flip by, my thoughts are not with home, or the blurry night of mistakes, or bodies that touched, tasted, and penetrated each other. My mind is already pointed west. I'm ready to leave by the time we go. Everyone wishes for a clean slate at some point in their life, and when that wish is paired with the fantasy of escaping poverty and the means to do so, it is particularly arresting.

Goodbye Reno. Goodbye desert. Goodbye history, poverty, life, and Anthony and eighteen years of figuring out how my parts fit together to make a complete person.

A day later, after travel and transfers and connecting with our basic training buddies in the Seattle airport, in processing offices, and orders and shuttle vans through a world we've never seen before, Viggy and I part, and perhaps I should have seen this coming: we never really speak again. Viggy doesn't ever really speak to anyone he met the nights before, and honestly, neither do I. I stay in touch in an American soldier sort of way, sporadic emails and brief updates over expensive calls home, but it doesn't take long for *home,* and everyone therein, to slip from a place to a memory.

Behind her door, she kept another boyfriend.
She kept him in the spring time, in the early month of May.
And if you asked her why the heck she kept him
She kept him from her soldier who was far, far away.

In Reno, one is constantly surrounded by hills. The city rests trapped between the Sierra Nevadas and the Virginia Range. It is a desert, tucked in the rain shadow of the mountains to its west. In the valley, one can see the evergreen pines coloring the mountains, but only the muted sagebrush decorates the sand tones of the city. In the midst of this drabness, the city's primary colors are neon and green. The skyline, where one would expect to find towers of office buildings in a city of this size, is made up of hotel-casinos, great monuments to the industry that drives the local economy. At night, they brighten the valley with luminous lines drawn in the night sky. In the end though, not even the shine of capital resists fading beneath the desert's inescapable light. Photodegradation touches everything: billboards and building exteriors, car paint and cowboy hats. Beneath the bastard sun, every-thing inches toward the wash of the sagebrush. It is a super-human task to keep anything looking new or clean in the city. To be out in the daylight is to damage oneself.

In Reno, one supports themselves by packing boxes, by building on a line, by serving drinks, by serving skin, by changing coin, by changing sheets. "We're crossing our fin-gers for that Tesla plant," my brother tells me between shifts unloading food in a freezer.

In Reno, one brother gets married and the other has chil-dren. My cousin does both. My father sobers up after chest pains put him in a hospital. Tabby finds her dream job cut-ting hair. Pearl joins the army to get away too, then marries a soldier and has his kid to get out of uniform. Alexis and her squad of children live in the sort of cluttered house that she grew up in. That I grew up in. That I fled. I don't talk to any-one from home now. Annie, the girl who waited, did not wait long. She met a guy, then a girl, and I met a girl, and a guy, and another girl. We pretended for a while, thought the romantic idea of a long-distance love between a soldier and his girl was worth carrying the weight of being dishonest, but eventually, balancing several lives stopped being worth it. Eventually, she left town, but made it back after a few years in Vegas. Reno is a basin: everything finds its way back to the bottom.

I don't know any of those friends any more. I don't know Reno, or the snow-capped Sierras, or the north valleys, those punchline suburbs of a punchline city. The next time that I stop in town, over a decade later and only then as a pit stop during a cross-country trip, I see as few people as I can man-age. I stay as briefly as I can. Reno is a basin, and I am still terrified of being trapped in its earthworks.

No more cadence counts (Oohh)
I want my forty ounce (Oohh)
Hey heyyyyy
We're going home.

It takes a transformation to stay away, but it takes something else too: distance. The same sort of distance writers talk about needing to see a subject or event clearly. Merely leaving Reno gave me the distance I needed to believe that I could leave. Not only to leave the sagebrush and the warm air, but to escape the orbit that keeps people in the city, that keeps people thinking that it's not so bad on the western edge of the Silver State. There's a quote from Fitzgerald that I find myself often returning to: "A clean break is something you cannot come back from; that is irretrievable because it makes the past cease to exist." That is what I was looking for when I left home, and also when I left the military, that vivisection of one life and the next.

I left the military during a particularly cold winter in Washington, D.C. As the snows came down, I found myself unlacing my boots for the last time, and by the time the thaw arrived, I worked for an LGBT nonprofit in the polished Dupont Circle neighborhood of the nation's capital. The glassy surfaces and floor to ceiling windows were the furthest I could get from returning to the casinos and dusty foothills of Nevada. It was my irretrievable break. I did not want to be a bootstraps story from Reno. I wanted that Anthony to cease to exist. I wanted to be a historyless figure with only his future ahead of him. Only joy, only shine. Brunches with mimosas. Business travel. Happy hours and keeping eyes open for the next big break.

So when my colleagues spoke about the past, over overpriced drinks in bars where all the shirts have collars and all the pockets have business cards, I spoke in ambiguities. I passed as someone who belonged by mimicking, just as we all do on occasion. That is how you dress for visitors. That is how you dress for drinks. This is when you are honest. This is when you are not. I aimed to be a blank slate, a Standard American success with no history and no heritage.

Reno leaves a stain though: imperfect manners and teeth, a constant state of apprehension about what I should and should not know. Tattoos that demand long-sleeved shirts. I notice when my measures of success get counted as "settling" by those who grew up expecting Ivy League success. I stand out here, or, at least, I am convinced that I stand out. The rules are different here, and I'm learning them mid-pitch.

Here even the horizon looks different; the sun rises in the east, over the sea, the origin of that brand-new golden light of morning, instead of a light that comes and goes behind the hills, the walls beyond which the rest of the world moves forward.

BACHELOR ENLISTED QUARTERS, CAMP CARROLL, KOREA

THE ROOMS were all the same: the layout, the furniture, the carpet, the fixtures. We would sign a receipt for each piece when we moved in so that the uniformity was by the numbers. If viewed from above, the rooms were z-shaped, with beds at each end, as far apart as we could get them. This was an attempt at privacy. Each room in the Bachelor Enlisted Quarters, the barracks where junior enlisted men and women housed, was a Spartan hotel room for two. Bed, wooden x2. Mattress, twin x2. Nightstand, wooden x2. Wardrobe, wooden x2. Refrigerator, x1 (shared). Microwave, x1 (shared). Each room was uniform, yet in our own way, each of us found a way to a room of our own.

In Seth's room, pages torn from fitness magazines with pictures of half-dressed men hung on the walls. The shots showed body builders he admired, oiled and flexing and wearing either skin-tight shorts or bikinis. He knew all of their names, their titles, their feats. Something about Seth, the way he carried himself, the way he spoke, left no space to suggest that this interest was anything but wholesome and heterosexual. His gaze was not my gaze. As in a lot of other rooms, the top of Seth's fridge was decorated with opaque plastic drums of whey protein and creatine powder. The stout, black canisters were a staple of the barracks; they would hang around for weeks after they were emptied, when we'd upcycle them into piggy banks, or into plastic helmets on drunken Saturday nights.

Danyel didn't let men into her side of the room. She didn't want to be seen as one of those types of army girls. Danyel didn't let women into her side of the room either. She didn't want to be seen as one of *those* types of army girls. When her peers got a chance to peek in from the doorframe, they might have noticed a photo of a gravestone tacked up above her pillow. They might have noticed a picture of a smiling, working-class mother with coarse hair and steelworker's arms. But these views were fleeting; her peers weren't invited in. Danyel didn't want to be seen as one of those types of army girls.

Cavendish was white and Midwestern. On his wall, Cav hung posters of bikini-clad women posing on airbrushed import sedans, posters of guys smiling with jewel-encrusted mouth ornamentation that people called *grills* or *fronts* at the time. He had a tower of electronics plugged into polished speakers the size of milk cartons that he mounted on the sides of his standard-issue oak wardrobe. On top of the wardrobe were hats, all sorts of clean, new hats, with the animal icons of his favorite sports teams pointed toward the center of the room. On Cav's fridge were bottles. Handles. Fifths. Liters. ABV. MGD. VSOP. Old No. 7. They were rarely full, and only briefly.

Angel hung a silk sheet on a shower-curtain rod over her side of the room. She said its purpose was privacy, but she couldn't control its suggestiveness. Angel liked company. Angel liked being seen. Angel liked to feel as though she was close to somebody. Any body. Many of us would come to see her. Her bed was the focal point of the room, its standard-issue coarseness covered in another flat sheet of cheap silk. As a result of the drape, the room was always dim. It felt like a whisper in there. "I've got to be out of here by first formation." Boys always whispered on her side.

Mike kept his room neat during weekdays. He hung nothing on his walls, and even his laptop was lined up neatly with the corner of his desk. On the weekends the room transformed. The beds became couches in a lively drinking parlor; the remaining furniture was put into the closet or stacked at one edge of the room. We needed to make room for a cocktail bar, cases of cheap beer, and a ping-pong table dressed with red, plastic cups. On the weekends, the spot burn burn burned with drunken songs, with flirtation, with the bonding and chest beating of young men told that they were warriors. Mike loved being a host, and he'd turn down the music several times throughout the night to propose a toast. To friends, to families, to sweethearts back home. Not yet to those who can no longer raise their glasses. We were too young for that, like the war that kicked off that year. Fresh off the boat. Still thinking (some dreading, some hoping) that the fight would be over by the time we left there.

Moll never really settled into his room. He was still a part of the crowd; he drank on the weekends, cracked jokes in formation, but he didn't really like having his comrades visit his room. The silk comforter was the only decorative addition that even suggested that the room was occupied. He'd often lay atop the made bed, talking to someone back home whose gender the other guys in the unit would speculate about. He kept his gear neatly organized in the closet, his clothes, both military and civilian, in tightly folded piles in the wardrobe. One would have to look close, real close, to find the room's character. A beat up pair of All Stars lined up alongside his boots. Nail polish that he hid in his shaving kit beneath the sink. An album collection that ranged from *Nsync to the Ramones stacked in a bottom drawer. What was it that he wasn't telling them?

PHOTO: MK 19

IN THE PHOTO, you can barely tell which is which. One of us is squatting down atop a Humvee, pretending to point toward the horizon somewhere over your left shoulder. The other figure leans into the first, half emerged from the gunner's hole in the roof of the truck, gazing toward the same vista. Both figures are clad in camouflage uniforms, both topped by turtle-shaped helmets: K-pots, we call them. We call the gear we're wearing *Full Battle Rattle*: helmet, armored vest and a mesh ammo vest over that, black gloves, black boots, olive drab gas mask attached in a carrier. We're wearing bright green, cash green, safety glasses. I found them in a dust-covered box in the back of our storage Conex a week prior and passed them out to the other gunners in my squad. We started calling ourselves the Cash-Money gunners. This doesn't mean anything really, not to us. Cash-Money is just something we heard on the radio.

The truck, wide and squat, wears the same pattern as we do. It holds earth between the tread of its front tires, also pointed toward you. The windshield looks water-stained and dusty. Beside the figure half concealed in the truck, a gun is mounted and centered on the roof. You might miss that it is a gun; maybe to you it's just an odd metallic attachment to the truck, an antenna perhaps. You might miss that the perfect black circle near the top of the object is a barrel pointed your way. It's a grenade launcher, Mk 19. To us, it is used to hurl up to three hundred and seventy-five 40-millimeter grenades outward toward whomever we're told.

It's easy to miss that Danyel is the one next to the gun. You can't tell, but she has silky brunette hair that she hides under a brown rag beneath her K-pot. The bottom half of our faces, below the glasses, is the only flesh exposed in the photo. You can almost tell that we're smudged with dirt here. Danyel doesn't mind; she loves to smother her clear skin with camo whenever we're out at training events like this anyway. My hair, under the helmet, is cut in a high-and-tight, a rectangle of uniform fuzz atop an otherwise closely shaven head.

You can't see any of this though, can't tell that she's a woman, can't tell that we're both queer. You can't tell one of us from the other. It is all blurred by the uniform: features, gender, personality, history. The purpose of camouflage isn't to make a person disappear, but to break up the silhouette that makes the figure recognizable as a person.

Look closer. Squint. When you get to the details, that's when the illusion begins to unravel. The green, metal box attached to the gun is hollow, offering only empty space where a can of ammunition should be. There's no driver in the driver's seat. There's no one in the truck at all. The figures in uniform: we're just nineteen-year-old kids, fresh from working-class homes. If you look closely enough, you might see a smirk. We're safe, playing. We don't yet know about America's longest war, still hot, fresh, and 3,000 miles away from us here. We don't yet know about loss.

When you squint, you also see that we're too young, not even old enough to drink. It's hard to tell because of how we're dressed. Because we're in the uniform of aggressors. Because you're staring down the barrel of a gun. Think of how many shots like this one exist; baby-faced soldiers posed alongside the instruments of war. It's almost always when we're young, isn't it? Photos from our first tour, photos from basic training. Before the newness of the experience wears off. When we are still full of pride, proud to be on our own, away from working-class homes, fighting for something we think we believe in. We're excited about new challenges. Excited about new toys. Excited to be soldiers, something different than before, anything but kids from Reno, kids from Gary.

PLUCKY AND DUMB

MILITARY BASES aren't like you imagine them. It's not all Jeeps and troops running together singing double-time cadences. They look like small towns. There are bars, gyms, bowling alleys, department stores. The buildings are more lackluster, the flags a bit wavier, but the image should be familiar to those who've seen small towns around the U.S.

I stood in the food court when it happened, in my gym clothes, my stripling arms folded over each other. I stood among the rows of unremarkable gray tables, slack-jawed, looking upward at the television overhead, as the sour smell of fast-food meat wafted from the nearby Burger King. On our provincial U.S. military base in South Korea, we were sure that the war would be done by the time we got back to the States.

Everyone looked up to the television overhead as a man from Texas told the world that a man from Al-Awja and his sons must abdicate and go into exile, lest his land face an invasion.

The young delivery driver slipped his bag onto the polished linoleum, and the graying, Korean woman who worked

the Baskin-Robbins stepped around from behind the counter
to listen to the president speak.

> *"Their refusal to do so will result in military conflict, com-
> menced at a time of our choosing."*

When I was younger, much younger, I pictured soldiers
learning about the start of a new war in formation: the cliché of a green-suited, star-shouldered leader pacing before
row after row of grave-faced men, giving them the hard news
seasoned with heroic rhetoric. That motivational pre-battle
speech those raised with film are so familiar with: George
C. Scott in *Patton*. Bill Pullman in *Independence Day*. Mel
Gibson in, well, several of his films.

> *"I want you to remember that no bastard ever won a war
> by dying for his country. He won it by making the other
> poor, dumb bastard die for his country."*

In early 2003, less than a year out of basic training, still
plucky and dumb, I anticipated that we would soon wind
down the war in Afghanistan. A comrade who grew up wanting to be a warrior told me earlier that month that he joined
hoping that he'd have a chance to take the fight to "those
bastards who took down our towers." Somehow, I felt embarrassed when I told him that I hoped he never got the chance.

In the days that would come, after he heard the news
about Iraq, my friend would share with me, over bottles in
the barracks, that he didn't understand why we were starting
this war when we hadn't finished the last. These late-night
confessions contrasted with the chest beating that would
take place during the day. Those of us new to the ranks
seemed to hold our breath; the anxiety of what it would
mean to start another war followed us wherever we went.
This was not true of the old heads, the sergeants, many of
whom had invaded Iraq a decade earlier. They were eager.

They talked about unfinished business and "that tyrant Saddam." Remembering the swiftness of the first invasion, the sergeants talked about how they hoped there would be some left for them after their tour in Korea was through. We young soldiers, we millennials, did not.

In the days that would come, the TV told us that in Seoul, a few hours up the road, 2,000 people protested the president's speech to the sounds of drums. 80,000 marched in Dublin. 300,000 in Berlin. 50,000 and a die-in in Boston. In Oakland, police deployed anti-riot arms against anti-war protestors. They marched in Paris, in London, in Moscow. They marched in both Israel and in Palestine. They marched in Christchurch and Buenos Aires, in Yemen and Kiev. And they marched into the history books: in all, the global community organized the biggest peace rally in the history of protest. Rounding out global opposition to the war on every continent, a small group of scientists even protested at the South Pole.

There, in front of the TV, even the nearby sergeant dressed in his fatigues, eating his golden french fries, shook his head to himself as the broadcast played. As the president continued, those of us near the TV remained hushed. The janitor ceased mopping. The cashier translated for the fry cook. All gazed upward toward the screen and remained arrested by the words for several moments after he ceased. A new war had begun.

There, in front of the TV, I was young. Someday, in the coming years, I would look back at these days and realize that they were the moments that cracked me open, the first leak of a dam certain to come apart. Though at that instant, I was still just selfish and American.

My brittle voice chipped at the silence. "I'm supposed to start leave tomorrow," I offered to no one in particular, my most immediate concern spilling out before strangers. The ice cream woman glanced at me, then turned and said nothing as she returned to her register. The delivery driver muttered to himself as he shuffled out the door to his car. The janitor continued his mopping.

WRONG AS TWO BOYS, PT. II

WHEN PEOPLE ASK how we knew, and people always ask, I tell them that we simply *figured it out.* In an army that told us we could not say "I'm queer," we found ways to say it with our eyes, our lips, our bodies. We found ways to stretch a gaze as long as it could be pulled, or to navigate the narrow alleys of femininity available to men in uniform. We found a way to communicate: an imperfect, unapproved way of telling, and, by extension, a silent way of asking.

Els noticed me when my voice broke in basic training, where I attempted to swell my courage enough to respond to the unchecked use of the word *faggot.* In the still-ruffled aftermath of a group fight that rang through the basic training barracks, Els found a way to quietly ask me, directly. I responded, in my very first attempt at closeted discourse, with the painfully awkward:

"I don't *not* like guys."

My words were enough. His hands were in my shorts, and I found myself being touched by a man for the first time. We felt our way through a nearly noiseless encounter in a closet, and then said nothing about the night ever again.

A few days later, under threat of being found out by our drill sergeants (or worse, our peers), I slipped wordlessly into his bunk in the earliest hours of the day, before sunrise, before even a stir from his bunkmate. Before our comrades rose to—as we were encouraged to say—*shit, shower, and shave,* I laid on his chest, squeezing into a twin-size top bunk, beneath a scratchy wool blanket, listening to his heart slam against his chest. It lasted no longer than a few minutes, not long enough for anyone else to chance by, and certainly not long enough for us to comfortably fall asleep, so we chose instead to obsess over every sound, every whispered vibration that slipped through the barracks halls, until the thought of danger demanded that I slink back to my own bunk.

After it all, we simply moved apart, as silently as we moved together, never speaking of the event again, never exchanging numbers or emails as we departed to our units. A silent few moments were all we needed. This was among the foundational lessons of my Army Basic Training: the silent ways in which we find ourselves needing to communicate, surrounded by an unknown threat.

"I was as Out as I could be," I tell folks, by which I mean that I did a poor job hiding the fact that I dated men, or that I vocally opposed the policy that said we must lie about our romances. It meant that I did not hide the fact that I spent summers attending Pride events, that I stuck a sticker on my car to support SLDN, the organization leading the charge on repealing the policy, that I was comfortable speaking openly about the idea of same-sex desire, even if I was forced to speak in abstracts.

This was, in part, a negotiated defense. My caution kept me safe: safe from being thrown out and denied my benefits, but also safe from the violence of those pockets of soldiers who carried the weapon of homophobia, a hatred allowed to go unchecked by an organization that could ignore those impacted by such prejudice. Speaking abstractly kept me physically safe when older enlisted men told me "just watch the friendly fire when these fairies go downrange" and "if I knew one of my soldiers was queer, I'd beat him to death."

Peaches did not share my sense of caution.

Peaches was flamboyant, the stereotype of a young, effeminate gay man. He didn't walk, or march; he floated from place to place, a delicate saunter punctuated by wrists bent in a mimicry of bourgeois femininity. Peaches was the sort of queer man that television loves to make a Gay Best Friend, and he moved with the type of swish that acts like a matador's cape for hyper-masculine American men.

Except that Peaches wore combat boots. The young twink was a tanker, a warrior trained to ride a 62-ton cavalry into battle. Peaches was trained to do damage, and he found no conflict between this identity and his delicate temperament.

Because he stood out from a crowd, I didn't have to do much work to identify Peaches as another queer soldier. He had a reputation. Everyone from the military police to the post commander knew of "that gay tanker." The first time I saw him, I matched the man to the reputation, but, through a moment of prolonged eye contact, Peaches figured me out almost instantly too.

"I just joined to meet men," he told me, laughing over a mojito, just minutes after meeting me in the on-base nightclub. Peaches brought me a drink and began chatting me up. Within minutes he had told me that I was handsome. He told me that he was considering doing military-themed porn down the highway in Van Nuys, the longtime pornography capital of the U.S. He told me that he shared a barracks room, but he could have the room empty on short notice. Peaches' flamboyant candor wasn't desperation; it was an act of unparalleled bravery. Honestly, he wasn't at all my type—not punk enough, not meaty enough, not rough enough around the edges—yet within a few weeks, he had

brought me to his barracks room. He surprised me by showing that he preferred to top.

After our encounter, he began to whisper to other soldiers, who would whisper to other soldiers, about the police
officer that he was fucking. Within a few weeks, my sergeant, a hard-nosed Latina who had come up among ranks
of hardened men, called me into the parking lot behind the
police station for a discussion. I could tell from the unchar-
acteristic warmth in her voice that something was amiss.

"Moll," she began, firmly, but unsure how to start. "I
need to talk to you about something. Relax a bit." We leaned
against the sand-colored walls of the station, looking over
the rows of police vehicles parked before us. "There are
these rumors going around, and, listen, I don't know if they
are true, and I don't want to know if they are true."

I knew then what it was we were discussing, and my
throat sank into my stomach.

"It's just . . . let me start again. You know Peaches, right?"

I tightened, unsure how to proceed.

"Yes," I stuttered. "Yes, Sergeant."

"The thing is, there are these rumors going around, and,
well, you're free to do what you want, but you've got to be
careful, you know?"

"Yes, Sergeant."

"I mean careful. Discreet, you know?"

"I know, Sergeant."

"I can't ask you what happened, and I don't need you to
tell me, but you've got to be careful." As the word rolled out
for the third time, I tried to swallow what it meant. I returned
to the danger that had rocked in my stomach, the feeling that
had quivered my hands as I sulked down the Spartan hallway to the door of Peaches' barracks room. I recalled that at
any moment my desire could be folded into violence.

"The thing is," she paused, shifting off the wall and
straightening the tight creases in her camouflage uniform.
"The thing is, Moll, we can't have rumors going around
about the company having a gay military police officer. You

have got to be careful. Do you really want to be known as 'that gay MP'?"

★

I worked long nights. Being a police K-9 handler for the U.S. Army meant shift work, and, being the new guy on the team, I was frequently the one left to strap on my belt for the overnight shift. This mostly meant driving in a circle for hours with a dog in the backseat of a patrol vehicle. Shift work also meant that I missed out on a lot of barracks parties, which meant that I would instead swing by while working, ostensibly to make sure everything was in order. Of course, the visits were to subdue my fear of missing out, and to be seen looking cute in uniform.

This isn't really a story about a boy. This is a story about a girlfriend.

"Hey, babe," Sara, the woman I had been seeing for the last few months, shouted from across the wide-open lawn as I arrived. Like everyone else there who wasn't in uniform, she was holding a red plastic cup and smiling. Sara moved her short, athletic body toward me; she offered me her crooked smile and wide eyes as she hurried to tell me some news. Sara bought into a certain idea of professionalism about being military police, so even in her excited state, she resisted hugging me while I was armored in my utility belt and Kevlar vest.

"His name is Tommy," she blurted, half whispered, with her drawn-out Tennessee accent.

I stared back without recognition.

"That boy! The one you told me you thought was cute and interested in you." Sara grinned and flipped her shoulder-length hair over to rest on one shoulder.

When we met a few months before, she seemed apprehensive about having a bisexual boyfriend, but part of her seemed intrigued by my attraction to men. Now, several months in, she got excited any time we discussed the topic. A week earlier, I mentioned to her that I had chatted with some new guy—a thin, neat boy from Kansas, just out of medic school and a bit shy. Tommy and I had spoken for almost an hour before the other medics from his squad dragged him away from a party I had thrown.

"I've been talking to him all night, and I think you're right about . . . you know."

"*About . . . you know,*" I teased back. "And how did you arrive at that?"

"He's just, he's just so sweet," she sipped from her cup between sentences. "And he's polite, and kind, and . . . I don't know. He's cute."

I smiled, nodding in agreement.

"You go get back to work, Specialist Moll. I'll bring you up to date on everything when you get home in the morning."

The mornings never came quickly. After a round through the lawn in front of the barracks building for high fives and *be safes,* I went back out to the Jeep, where my dog Johnny slept quietly, as tired and as bored as I was, working on a Friday night. We drove and drove, circling the quiet desert base for hours on a particularly quiet night, bearing the top-40 music laced with PSAs that rang from the on-base radio station. We drove until that silent hour, after the parties died, before the sun rose, when Johnny could eat and rest in his kennel, and I could turn over my pistol and head home.

I flipped through my keys as I approached my barracks room. I rarely expected to come home to an empty bed. Because I was in a special unit, I was lucky to have a room to myself, but Sara had been staying over more and more frequently lately, choosing to share a bed with me instead of a dorm with her roommate. As I grabbed the door handle, Sara spoke hurriedly from behind the door.

"Hold on—hold on for just one second," she ordered from behind the door. "I've got a surprise for you!"

I paused, puzzled, expecting her to be asleep at this hour, huddled in the king-sized nest I had created by pushing the two full-sized, standard mattresses into a single unit.

"*Now* come in," she called from inside, mischief trilling her voice.

When I entered, tossing my belt and vest onto the couch, I found Sara smiling from the pile of pillows and comforters, wearing her matching panties and camisole set, cuddled next to a thin, shirtless boy from Kansas.

"Hi," he murmured as he smiled at me. "Sara told me that she wanted to do something nice for you."

I nearly tumbled over as I raced to take off my boots. We were young, and we were striking, and we were careless. There was kissing, and touching, and, as often happens in group situations, the lines between bodies became blurred. Because this sort of thing was not only frowned upon by the U.S. military, but also actually illegal, there was law breaking in the military police barracks until just before dawn, when we began to navigate the delicate politics of cuddling.

Those who engage in bed sharing of any type regularly know that managing the space of two people in a bed is difficult enough. Managing three is a circus. In situations like this, everyone finds themselves navigating their own comfort, the expectations of how nice everyone hopes it to be, and the social dynamic between each person involved.

"I don't want to be on the outside," I told them as I slipped my boxer-briefs back over my butt.

"Well, no one wants to be on the outside."

"I don't mind being on the outside," Tommy offered, still blushing at the edge of the bed.

"At least two people need to be on the outside."

"How about I spoon you, and he spoons me?"

"Oh, I don't want to be a big spoon."

"At least two people will need to be big spoons too."

Before the pile finally settled, Tommy, who was convinced to be the big spoon closest to the light switch, turned the room dark and nuzzled up behind me.

The first light had already begun to shine through the curtains. Soon the rest of the military base would wake. Soldiers would be running in formation. The speaker playing a reveille horn would sound. The buzz of day would return.

We packed tightly together, so it was only minutes before the heat of three people cuddling became too much.

"I changed my mind. It's too hot. I don't want to be in the middle."

A feminine sigh sounded in the dark.

"I think that I'm just going to go," Tommy murmured. "This was nice, but . . . I'm just going to go." Sara and I sat up and made a half-hearted offer for him to stay as he pulled on his jeans and T-shirt. "This was great though. Maybe do all this again some time?"

We did not. I didn't talk much to Tommy after that night, despite the fact that he was just my type. We would nod to each other at barracks parties, maybe even say hello every now and then, but the truth was that the night wasn't for us. We realized afterward, maybe we even realized the night it happened, that those early morning hours were about an idea, an adventure, a story we could tell down the line, not because the experience was magical, but because each of us would make it part of our mythologies. The night was about a young woman excited to bind three bodies together in the type of story that each will whisper about for years.

The military provided me with plenty of opportunities to meet men who were much more attractive than me. Martinez was no exception. He looked simply beautiful, from his perfectly groomed eyebrows to his flawless smile to his meticulously cared-for body. He was smart too, an army medic training to be a registered nurse. And he was brave: gay men's magazines were displayed prominently on the end tables of his consistently spotless barracks room.

He was the first man to show me how to live openly, even when muzzled. There was no need to resolve "is he or isn't he" with Martinez. The medic *was,* and if anyone wanted to throw him out because of it, he knew the army needed med-ics more than he needed the army.

"You just keep these out?" I asked, fingering through the stack of glossy issues of *Advocate* and *OUT* on his night-stand.

"Sure, why wouldn't I?"

"You don't have inspections come through?"

"I do. My sergeant came through here just last week."

"And?"

"And he tried to tell me to be careful, and I told him that I had no need to be careful about the material I choose to read."

"Christ."

I watched Martinez as he navigated parties—he never wore his queerness as a costume. Unlike me at the time, unlike Peaches, Martinez knew who he was. He wasn't try-ing to pass as straight in some hyper-masculine way, either—somehow, in his mid-20s, he had already resolved the questions of masculinity, desire and identity that so many of us were still stumbling through. Even then he resisted the assimilationist politics of "we're just like you." The other queer soldiers brought their flamboyance to parties, wore it so they could fly the flag for those looking for it. But Marti-nez sipped his beer, smiled at the men he wanted to smile at, and talked openly and honestly about everything, just short of saying the words we all knew we could not say.

And one day he smiled at me. We never slept together. I wasn't that to him. He was something to me, though: a moment, a comrade, a model for living. He was one of many men I would meet over the years who I stole a tiny bit from, a small piece of being that would help me complete the puzzle of what it means to be oneself, queer and whole.

SISTERS IN THE PRESENCE OF STRANGERS, PT. I

IN THE final chapter of an academic text on queerness, Michael Snediker explores the friendships that can exist between queer people of different genders. He discusses the radical possibility of queer literature to fill the gap that queer theory has thus far ignored—the love that can exist between a queer man and a queer woman. This love represents a radical possibility—it erases the heteronormative nonsense that men and women cannot be friends, that the best way for men and women to build something together is procreation. For me, these sorts of friendships have long been an act of survival, and they were the ones the lingered even after almost a decade of the transient military life.

Dany
Dany was probably my first real friend in the army, in part, because I wasn't trying to fuck her.

Private First Class Danyel Claire was the sort of young soldier for whom the term *squared away* was invented. She loved firing the machine gun, and she did it better than anyone else in the squad. Her lean body ran and marched as well, or better, than any man in the squad. She spent her downtime with training manuals and books on military history in her lap, and she knew her way around maintaining both a rifle and our armored trucks. Danyel navigated the world with a determined stare and her head high, in part because a certain fierceness is expected of young military police, and in part because she was resisting the fact that many of the men who surrounded her saw Dany as a beautiful woman first, and as a soldier second.

We met briefly my first night in the barracks, when an unofficial welcoming committee snatched me up as soon as I entered the building and pulled me into a party. It was the first night of many parties, the start of a months-long rotation of long days and hard-drinking nights.

Most people make friends quickly in these sorts of units—it's hard not to, spending all day working or training with the same 20 folks before shuffling back to the barracks where you all live. Those ties bind quickly, especially when everyone is thousands of miles away from home for the first time.

Danyel kept her distance though. She was only an occasional visitor to the barracks parties, stopping in to say hi before heading back to her barracks room or sneaking out to the bars with the young noncommissioned officers.

When we weren't drinking, we were finding ways to stay busy that we wouldn't normally try. Some soldiers picked up video game controllers for the first time, some tried hiking, which was more enjoyable during our off time, when we weren't in combat boots and thirty-five-pound ruck sacks. I tried football. Coming from a background of going to raves and punk shows between playing Dungeons & Dragons with my friends, I did not have much success.

After some shoving, and some shit talking, and some soldiers holding each other back, I found myself walking off the field offering my middle finger to those behind me and holding in tears, tears I wouldn't dare let the other soldiers see.

Danyel found me in the stairwell a few minutes later, where the tears had finally made their way to my face.

"I can't stand that word," I pushed out between sobs. "Those motherfuckers can't say that word."

"*Faggot?*"

I nodded, attempting to snort the sobs back into my body.

"Moll, dudes are going to say stuff like that. You can't let it get to you."

"Then I am going to keep getting into fights."

"You can't fight every asshole in the Army."

"I just—I joined because I thought all of this would flatten that out, you know? I thought all of this hoorah stuff would knock that sort of bullshit out of place."

The army is not an intimate place. It is an *intimately close* place—soldiers sleeping nearly on top of each other, sharing showers, packing tightly into military vehicles—but the emotional closeness that should occur finds itself muted by humor: fart jokes, gay jokes, sack taps. Like so much of America, soldiers find themselves unable to engage with the sincerity that might offer a discomforting honesty, even as the nature of the military draws the most American of fears to the surface—fear of dying alone.

Stumbling through what to say, I told Danyel that I liked men. I said the words, unlike most of the conversations I would have in the seven years that followed. For years I would sidestep the question, or I would suggest it without saying it. I knew what the rules said, and I did my best to work around them, but there were few people I actually said the words to. I told her with a sincerity that makes me blush to remember, about the "real me," and about trust and friendship. The conversation unfolded through the afternoon, and after a long time of talking and crying and revealing in a stairwell that smelled of cleaning products and wax, Danyel responded in kind.

"You know," she began, unsure how to proceed. "You know I like men—I mean—you know I'm seeing Rico, I just—" she tripped through it too, the cliché phrases, the uncomfortable sidestepping, but she was looking for honest words.

"Women are just so beautiful! I don't know what that means, but, it means something, right?"

That was the start of it, she became the first person that I came out to in the army, and I became the first person she ever came out to anywhere. The rest we would learn as we go, the shitty cities we came from, the reasons for leaving home, how to be friends for each other after messy breakups. We'd take each other to our first gay club. Hold hands as we got our first tattoos in a shop where they had to lock the doors. We'd watch each other flirt, watch each other fail to flirt, watch each other get sick after nights of drinking and dancing, but to start, we just said the words.

Bea

"Gimme that motherfucker," Bea told us as she snatched the oversized glass from the center of the ring of cards. "If I am going to do this, I'm going to do it quick."

I didn't expect this boldness from the woman I had met just an hour prior. Bea's slight frame and uncomfortable extraversion would never have suggested the fearlessness of the woman I would come to consider one of my closest friends. That night she arrived at the barracks with a friend of a coworker who knew that our unit had become the place to party on base. Yet with a looming holiday and most of the unit working overnight shifts, she arrived on a fairly quiet night. Even quiet nights were drinking nights at that age though, so we found what booze we had on hand in our refrigerators and decided to make an event of it.

Our barracks were a lot like a dormitory. We'd drink and we'd flirt and we'd find silly games to help us navigate socializing with other people our age. Beer pong. A card game named Asshole. Flippy cup. That night we laid ourselves out on the carpet in front of the couch and played a game in which each card pulled had a player take a drink or pour whatever they were drinking into a cup in the center of our ring of bodies. When a player pulled the last king of the deck, that player drank the amalgam that had been created in the communal cup.

Bea pulled the last king.

"Oh shit!"

"All you, Bea."

Bea did not make eye contact with the men around her who were convinced that she would not touch the cup she was set to drink, the men who were sure that she would find a way out of it. She looked directly at the cup, wrapped her hands around it, and brought it to her lips, lifting its base high into the air as she swallowed twenty ounces of sweet malt liquor, cheap beer, apple-flavored liquor, and scotch.

She slammed the glass back down on the carpet.

"What's next?"

Over the next few weeks, Bea would become a staple at parties, a heavy drinker with an ache for adventure. She made out with men and women in the corners of parties with little concern for what the rules said, and because the people we partied with almost universally adored her, she had no need to worry. Even when a drunk friend intentionally burst in on her riding another friend of ours in a barracks room near where we partied, and she responded by hurling a full beer bottle at his head, most of us sided with her, scolding the off-duty military police officer on what a jerk he had been.

Bea and I grew together. She convinced me to get back into running, and I reminded her she wasn't a bad person when a colleague lectured her about the men she dated. I did my best to be there for her during the summer of her abortion, simply sitting with her in a cold barracks room and watching cartoons as she repaired herself. We were there to cry on each other when John was taken from us, first to the desert and then from the world. We navigated our early twenties together, growing from young adults into something new, growing from strangers into siblings.

Michelle

The building where our unit's administrative offices were found—where the company commander and first sergeant sat in their offices, where those soldiers with clerical jobs were posted—looked unremarkable. Like many buildings on military installations, it was built to be that way. A sand-colored exterior. An earthy brown roof. Everything nondescript, nothing standing out.

Inside—where the wood-panel walls were decorated with unit insignia and portraits of the unit's chain of command, extending from our unit commander to the President of the United States—I was introduced to the junior soldiers for the first time just days after I arrived.

"This is Sergeant Moll," the platoon sergeant told the handful of enlisted soldiers sitting on the couches in the main room. "He's coming from Korea, and he'll be with us here at headquarters for a few months."

The soldiers eyed me up and down. All of them were junior to me, and I would be a team leader for a few of them, but they glanced my way with the suspicion any group has of new members.

"Where you coming from, Sergeant?"

"Korea, my second trip."

"No combat patch, Sergeant?"

"Nope, I've been in Korea, California, and Korea again."

The soldiers shared a glance with each other.

"You're supposed to be our guy for the NCO of the Year thing, Sergeant?" The twenty-something woman looked at me. She carried a weight on her face, not angry, just heavy. Heavy from a combat deployment and the weight of being a woman in the military, of being told what women cannot be, cannot do, should not think.

"That's right, Specialist. That's what they tell me."

In that ordinary moment, there was a recognition, however brief, in each other's voices. Maybe it was the pitch, or the softness, or the tone of quiet anger hummed into determination. Maybe the recognition didn't arrive as a tone, but in the way we each carried ourselves through the world, through the world of military life in particular. However it was that we noticed, we did so subtly, in the invisible in-between that queers learn how to read early, the super power that popular culture likes to call "gaydar."

A few weeks later, in the same boring building, a few days after she heard me speak up during a bullshitting session with the other sergeants that moved toward the topic of "the gays" serving openly in the military, Michelle would ask me if I knew anything about Baltimore. She would ask me if I knew the civilian police officer who worked on base, the one who she went to bars with in Baltimore. She would ask me if I knew about the Mt. Vernon neighborhood in Baltimore, where she would go for drinks with the civilian police officer who worked on base.

She would go on to introduce me to the city where Poe died, and its gay bars, and a group of lesbians who would become my family for a short time, taking me in and showing me what a queer city life in Baltimore could be like, still new to me, fresh after a year and a half overseas.

"This is Tony," she shouted to the group over the booming dance music. "I can call you Tony, right?"

"I'm not sure that calling me Sergeant Moll would be appropriate in this setting."

She turned back to the group, sipping from her drink. "He's our new sergeant; he's going to be NCO of the Year."

"You work with Michelle?"

I nodded and shifted awkwardly on my barstool.

"And you're a gay?"

"Excuse me?"

The group burst into laughter, dancing along and drinking as they did so. "Relax, hon. You're among family."

Michelle offered me a drink and the group began to dance together. This became the place we would come to escape the grind of a military police unit where old timers would tell us that they would retire whenever the gays were let in, where they'd tell us that women shouldn't be tattooed, or deep voiced, or veterans of combat, where they'd tell us that queers risked friendly-fire if they were Out during deployment. Here at the gay bar we would argue about politics— me a leftist and her a libertarian—as we drank and danced to top 40: Rihanna, Fergie, and Gwen Stefani punctuating our discussion. Here I would not meet a single guy, but I would be surrounded by beautiful queer energy, backed by a tribe of lesbians who welcomed me with open arms. Here, Michelle and I would dance together, back to back with each other, apart from a military that told us we did not belong.

PHOTO: CEDANT ARMA TOGAE

THIS IS ONE of the last photos taken of him in the United States, one of the last photos taken while he was alive. It isn't the newsboy cap or the day-off scruff on his face that my eyes go to when I look at this one, it is John's pudgy frame wrapped in the kaleidoscopic bed sheets of his childhood.

He carried the sheets with him all along, from his small-town home to his first unit, the 82nd Airborne Division, American's premier unit of parachute-trained warriors. Then he packed the sheets alongside an armored vest, the baby wipes he used for field hygiene, and the mini-DVD player for boredom, as he left for the desert, his first combat tour, dusty, bloody, and inescapable, even for those who survived. They were tucked into his duffle when he came out west, here to the training base where the army sent him for a brief respite after an ugly tour. Here out west he could breathe for a moment, the desert climate of Southeast California not unlike his first trip to war, but the volume turned down, a community temporarily removed from the fighting. Here out west we all could forget for brief periods that we were warriors for a nation constantly fighting, constantly sending our bodies around the world to shoot and be shot at.

The sheets are decorated with Transformers, the cars-turned-fighting-robots cartoon he watched as a boy. When we first discussed the toga party, many of us leapt toward elaborate ideas—some of us hand-sewed our togas from swaths of material bought just for the occasion, accessorizing with the toga sinus, or with plastic swords and shields. Some of us just snatched the sheets off of the twin-sized barracks beds: coarse, military issue or high-thread-count slips bought at the post exchange. John knew right away what he would wear: that faded, decorated sheet from back home.

In Rome, when it was more common attire, the toga was considered impractical for military use; the garment's loose folds made it difficult to run, or jump, or swing a weapon. Ancient Roman soldiers instead reserved the toga for their downtime, their leisure days between marches or during periods of peace. I would love to tell you that we wore our togas with this in mind, but our fascination more closely aligned with the association other early-twenties Americans have with the garment: the parties on college campuses across the U.S. Like those on college campuses, we wore the toga as a symbol of youth, as a symbol of fun, as an excuse to drink.

Except that John had spent twelve months of his college years surrounded by rifles, bullets, and sand, and within a few months, he would return to the desert. Except that half of the group had just returned from a year guarding men who were snatched from their country and flown to one of the most controversial prisons in the world, Guantanamo Bay. Except that we all carried the weight that many of us would leave again soon, that some of us would never return.

The reason this photo is one of my favorites is that we had not yet gotten word of the deployment. The orange light shining a halo behind John is the first light of autumn, just before the orders came down, when we are still basking in a summer of forgetting about the streets of dusty desert towns and the gray ethics of a war few of us believe in. For a moment, we are children wrapped in sheets, college-aged

Americans clinking together brown bottles dripping with a condensation that reminds us how long our days still are.

He was twenty-two when he went again, when he packed it all up again: his sheets, the new truck bought with the money saved during the first deployment, the newsboy cap, the DUI charge he would never return to deal with, pictures from home, pictures from a summer when we were all still young and breathing.

ON RITUAL

THIS IS the story in every military memoir: the brother who didn't come back. In that sense, it is the story of every war: young men and women die for the plans of old men, and their comrades feel the ripple of each death.

Those who read war stories know that these narratives aren't about war. They are about loyalty to one another, and about learning and growing, or they are cautionary tales futilely pushing back against the beat of the next war drum. The death of a comrade is a story that does all of this, and it outlines the shape of another familiar narrative: the love story. War literature is almost entirely love stories, and they are almost entirely queer. Where one doesn't find love easily classified as sexual or romantic, one finds homosocial love. The ritualistic mourning of the fallen is queer in that it is one of the few places acceptable in our society for men to weep openly over the death of another man who is not related by blood or marriage. To be tender when you are told to be stone, to make visible the loss of those who history loves to forget: that is queer ritual.

Military life is one filled with ritual, from the oath of enlistment to separating from the military. Notwithstanding special circumstance, there are two ways one expects to leave the military: on his feet or on his back. The former is routine, but when one leaves the military in the worst way, the ritual is grand and recursive. This is something soldiers learn along the way, but even as they begin their service, a sense of ritual and sacrifice touches everything. Scholars call the rituals of transition from one period of life to another life-crisis rituals. This category includes births, initiation and rites of passage, death, and departures.

Imagine the DMV. Imagine the hospital. Imagine the civil servants you've met who want only to perform a rote task for eight hours and go home with a paycheck, who make no disguise of their complete disregard for your concerns or your joys.

This is the Military Entrance Processing Station, MEPS. This is where it begins.

My recruiter drops me off here on Saturday morning in a minivan with an Army of One decal plastered across the side. I wouldn't have suspected this building; it's an office building, low and flat and unremarkable, not an army base. There are no tanks, no jets, no troops running in formation. At this point, I don't yet know a thing about the military. My understanding of military service at the time comes from '90s television shows about the army—until a few days ago, I thought that the whole military still slept in cots and hammocks inside of cluttered tents.

We start the first day testing: they want to see how smart I am or am not, what I might be good at. Later, we get a physical. Background checks. Filling in bubbled forms. Standing in line and waiting in seats. *Imagine the DMV. Imagine the hospital.* For those of us who live in other cities, or outside of cities, our recruiters leave us here for the weekend. They put us up in a hotel for the night, so we can do it all at once.

On the medical side of the building, a breathalyzer is included in the process, a urine test too. This is the end of the line for many participants.

We see the contract officer, who tells us what jobs are available, and when we can leave. I'm frightened, and eager, and ignorant, so I tell him I want to ship out quickly. My recruiter, who can't be here, warned me that this is the person who will hardball me. My recruiter, who can't be here, told me what to tell them—be honest—and what to keep secret—arrests, medical concerns. My recruiter, who can't be here, is rated professionally on the number of boys and girls he enlists.

Toward the end, the walls of the room where we will enlist are covered in birch paneling, holding the seals of each branch of the military at eye level. We're not in uniform, and we don't yet know how to stand in straight lines, so a friendly man in army greens tells us where to stand. Despite his effort to organize, the room is still a muddle of hooded sweatshirts and T-shirts with logos. Jeans and flip-flops. Deep breaths and jitters.

Families and friends are asked to line the walls. Sisters take photos. Mothers try, unsuccessfully, to hold their tears in. Fathers wrap their arms around the family and hold their chin high with pride. They told us just before we entered how the oath will go, and what our options are.

"Attention to orders. Please raise your right hand."

"I, Anthony Moll, do solemnly affirm (or swear; yes, we are given the option) that I will support and defend the Constitution of the United States against all enemies, foreign and domestic; that I will bear true faith and allegiance to the same; and that I will obey the orders of the President of the United States and the orders of the officers appointed over me, according to regulations and the Uniform Code of Military Justice." (Optional, but preferred by most soldiers: So help me God.)

Applause. Tears. Unspoken too-late regrets.

"Troops, could you please file back into the next room. We've got contracts to sign to make it all official. Families, you can get your hugs and your kisses in a few minutes."

Life-crisis. The ritual is done. The sons and daughters will leave soon. They will change soon, many too quickly, some forever.

The families are changed too. They have given their children to Sparta. They can now wear the symbols of sacrifice, their yellow ribbons, their blue stars. Many of our history's earliest rituals revolve around sacrifice, gifts to entities, to gods and god-kings, to luck or fate. In a sense, these gifts are meant to appease the entity, but at their roots, this appeasement is based in an economy. The sacrifice is a trade. Something is given, something is earned.

In February 2002, I arrived at Fort Leonard Wood, Missouri, with dyed hair and naive pride. It was my first time on a plane, my first time away from home for more than a few days.

In June, seventeen weeks later, I left, twenty pounds lighter, with nothing but a newly grown patch of fuzz on top of an otherwise cleanly shaven head, as a member of the army that had recently invaded Afghanistan, that would soon invade Iraq.

Before we left, before we joined the Real Army, we held a ceremony. We marched, in unison, into an auditorium filled with loved ones. We stood erect in several lines on the stage, staring straight forward, trying not to bend our necks as our eyes scanned the audience for our families and sweethearts. A chaplain in his military Class-A uniform performed the invocation, *Please bow your heads*. A master of ceremony called our names one by one. A military commander talked about transformation and sacrifice. Someone said *call to service*. Someone said *freedom's frontiers*.

Ritual and myth are an interwoven presence in any culture. The military perpetuates a great many myths, both epic and mundane—freedom isn't free, fighting to protect your nation, the nation's highest calling. At their root though, these stories are mere distillations or revision of the oldest and ugliest myth—that slogan we cannot escape: *Dulce et Decorum est Pro Patria Mori.*

"Don't be a pussy about it."

No one ever wanted to be accused of "being a pussy about it." We took it. We earned the promotion, and the blood and bruises were part of the process. Call it hazing. Call it tradition. Call it rite of passage. I can't call this one queer ritual; this is more recognizable as heterosexual masculinity.

I stood at attention, my feet together, shoulders back, hands at my side, head and eyes straight forward. They leaned in one by one, congratulating me first, offering a handshake with a darkened smile.

When I wore Specialist, and Private First Class, our uniforms held the insignia by pinning it onto the lapel. The rank we acquired, its physical manifestation, a pin, replaced the old rank on the lapel where it rested on the collarbone. The backs of the pins (*butterfly clutch* most commonly, but *damn-its* to soldiers) were left off, exposing the sharp prick itself to the cloth just above the tender upper chest.

Sometimes it was just a slap. A firm smack on the rank. Sometimes it came as a punch, downward, with the bottom of the hand. Sometimes it was completely undisguised, a flat palm grinding the pin toward the flesh for several seconds. Sometimes there were several of us in a row—one would form an orderly line and perform the ritual to each member. No crying was allowed, nor attempts to avoid it, though generally, the hissing sound one makes by sucking air in through their teeth was permitted. Like so much of the military, this ritual is not permitted; officially it is even discouraged, but, in reality, it is widespread.

The army switched its uniforms beginning in 2004; the rank was no longer pinned to the lapel, but rather, attached by Velcro to the chest, near the tip of the sternum. The switch from a slap to a straight-fist punch to the chest quickly led to stories about broken ribs, fistfights and projectile vomiting at promotion ceremonies.

★

Beyond life-crisis, other common categories of ritual are imitative and sacrificial. We use these to exchange histories and culture, to bestow merit, to appease unseen entities, to express allegiance and share what is profane, what is divine.

"Please bow your heads as our Chaplain delivers the invocation."

The U.S. military begins most of its rituals with invocation. This is true not only of memorial observations, but for nearly all its rituals: inductions, graduations, promotions, Bon Voyage, Welcome Home, dining out, change of command, unit formation, and unit realignment. I've performed these rites more times than I can count. In my mind, the ceremonies blur together, and among all of them, there is one moment they all share: *Please bow your heads.*

And the soldiers do, sometimes dozens, sometimes hundreds, all together, standing in a line and dressed alike. Chins tuck into camouflaged shirts. Because I am not immune to the effects of this culture, I worry that others think *disrespectful* or *disobedient* as I remain staring straight forward, or in less formal situations, eyeing left and right, looking for another godless warrior. Every now and then, I catch the eye of another such soldier, and each pair of eyes asks the other: *Can you believe this?*

I realized early in my military career how green I was to believe in a secular military. Even in basic training, soldiers either marched to (primarily Christian) church services, or we spent Sunday mornings in the barracks with the drill sergeants. I was naive, but I wasn't stupid—I attended a different service each week to escape the barracks, even the non-Christian services, even the Wiccan observance, where I and one other recruit sat beneath a tree behind the barracks while a drill sergeant kept a watchful eye from his office a few hundred feet away. Officially, you can be any faith you'd like in the military, but it's easy to notice how easily the services that weren't Christian and Protestant became viewed as nonessential.

Regardless of which faith their dog tags listed, soldiers bowed their heads before being sworn in, and they bowed their heads when they graduated. Later they will bow their heads when commanders are changed and at formal dinners. Each ritual in the U.S. Army reminds its ranks, intentionally or otherwise, which unseen entity it is that those in charge want us to appease, to express allegiance toward.

The few military rituals that begin without invocation are those that one might describe as more "functional," or at least, having origins in a functional purpose. Reveille and Retreat, the hand salute, inspection arms. The latter of these is imaginatively nonfunctional, despite its original intent. From the manual for drill sergeants to teach young recruits the movement:

> Inspection arms from order arms is a seven-count movement. On the command of execution ARMS of Inspection, ARMS, execute port arms in two counts. On count three, move the left hand from the hand guard and grasp the pistol grip, thumb over the lower portion of the bolt catch. On count four, release the grasp of the right hand, unlock the charging handle with the thumb, and sharply pull the charging handle to the rear with the thumb and forefinger. At the same time, apply pressure on the lower portion of

the bolt catch, locking the bolt to the rear. On count five, without changing the grasp of the right hand, sharply push the charging handle forward until it is locked into position; then regrasp the rifle with the right hand at the small of the stock. On count six, remove the left hand, twist the rifle with the right hand so that the ejection port is skyward, regrasp the handguard with the left hand just forward of the slip ring, and visually inspect the receiver through the ejection port. On count seven, with the right hand, twist the rifle so that the sights are up and come to inspection arms.

All that is to say, a seven-count movement in which you lift a rifle from your side to the front of your face, and pull back the bolt to inspect for any ammo remaining in the weapon. As young recruits, we spent hours standing in uniform, in the Ozark wind of late winter, repeating this movement until we, as a unit of over two hundred, could perform the ritual not only with precision, but also in unison.

SNAP, a bolt would squeal metallically and out of turn.

"We'll be out here all damn day if we have to, Privates!"

We never thought to speak up, to ask why, when upon completion of this task, we would unceremoniously file past the clearing barrel, a sand-filled industrial barrel into which we would stick the muzzle of our rifle, pull back the bolt and inspect for any ammo remaining in the weapon, executing simply and functionally the task we had spent hours performing.

Most functional explanations of ritual attempt to explain this behavior in relation to the needs and maintenance of a society. If the need to clear the weapon is no longer part of the ritual, what is it then that we imitate? What is the function?

*

There is very little ritual for most enlisted soldiers when they separate from the military voluntarily and still breathing. I stood, with my hands behind my back for the final time, as my commander spoke to the gathering of those soldiers who were on duty that day inside of our dreary office space. The scene was one that would be familiar to many, despite our uniforms, as we gathered for a final round of hand shaking and well wishing.

"I know he'll go on to do great things, to make the army proud," my boss told the small crowd as he patted me on the back.

He handed me a plaque and we posed for pictures. Handshake hugs were made with excessively deliberate movements, masculine and awkward in their own way. This event was routine, down to the statement, yet it didn't move the same way as the rigid, formal process one sees in other rituals. There are no training manuals for send-offs. The act was something closer to a custom, a tradition handed down orally, imitatively.

My final day in the army—particularly warm and still for early December, when all the trees are barely scaffolding of their younger selves—I received a final signature, shared a few final goodbyes, and I slipped into my car and drove off base, unceremoniously, unremarkably really, leaving as a soldier for the final time.

When one leaves the military in the worst way, the ritual is grand and recursive.

John got the order to go back to the desert in early 2005. He told me, the week before they went, in twilight hours, from the bottom of a pint, he knew he wasn't coming home this time. May of that year, a homemade roadside bomb shredded through a Humvee John was driving through Iskandariyah, Iraq.

When we heard he was gone, gone for good, we had a memorial, and wake, and then a burial. It was a first for many of us, certainly for me. It was the first time that the message wasn't just "soldiers dying," or even "brothers-in-arms dying"; it wasn't rhetoric anymore.

John was dead.

John who told us to call him Pudge. John who hugged everyone when he got drunk. The same John who wore Transformers sheets to a toga party and drank straight from the pitcher.

At the memorial, a helmet and a pair of dog tags hung on a rifle standing barrel down behind an empty pair of tan boots. An officer gave the roll call memorial: *Smith. Sergeant John Smith. Sergeant John McClellan Smith.* The Chaplain told my buddies that John's favorite song, "Boys on the Docks," sounded too aggressive for the mood of the memorial, so we had an informal wake that night, the first of several that summer. The song played all season long. It played during late nights, when the pint glasses were full, and until they were empty. It played during drinks poured into the soil in memory of the fallen. We talked about the whole thing for years, always while drinking, and we always said *hero*. Soldiers always say *hero*, even when we have yet to resolve for ourselves what the word means. This is a gesture of love. This is loyalty. This is queer.

John was twenty-two during the twenty-one-gun salute. He is survived by his mother, who received a folded flag at his funeral. At the service, boys in uniform (the current roster of his high school's lacrosse team, wearing their jerseys) offered condolences to the family and to the public.

His obituary says that he always wanted to be a soldier.

They buried him near his grandfather, a veteran of the second war to end all wars.

PHOTO: CLUB SPOT

YOU WOULD NEVER guess that we were soldiers, the three of us, linked at the shoulders in the dimly lit club. We don't look like warriors, at least not in the sense that most people think when they imagine the soldiers and sailors of the U.S. military.

The grinning punk in the middle, the one who looks like a skinhead in his The Oppressed T-shirt and shaved head, is Van, and he is, without question, actually a skinhead. On the streets outside of punk venues like the one we're in here, where we sit on the curb drinking Korean beer and street vendor food, Van and the other skins have brought me up to speed on the misconceptions and finer points of "skin" culture. I am taught that the racist men who most Americans consider skinheads are considered "boneheads" by other skins, and that the roots of skinhead culture come from anti-racist and anti-fascist unity. Needless to say, the two factions do not always get along. For both groups, racist and traditional skins, music and clothing is a significant part of the culture, and because outsiders find little distinction between the sounds and threads of each, we often don't recognize the difference between the two. In the photo, where I am smiling and cheering with Van, I don't yet recognize that even as Van and the other skins explain this to me, he is very likely the racist type. It isn't until later that night, outside of the club in the blurry, post-club hours of Seoul's bustling streets, that I start to question which side Van resides on—as a group of Korean men surround and begin shouting at a multi-racial man outside of a nearby hip-hop club, Van barks over the din as the shoving begins, igniting the moment into chaos, "Beat that filthy mongrel back to where he came from!"

In the photo, Ben, the half-Korean U.S. soldier linked under Van's other arm, doesn't yet know this about Van either. In his hooded sweatshirt over all-black clothes, Ben winces at the camera's bright flash. He isn't one for the sort of cheering Van and I are doing here in the photo, rowdy for one of our favorite local bands to take stage. Ben isn't what you might expect of a navy sailor or a punk rocker. He is thoughtful in everything that comes out of his mouth, dislikes the politics of the U.S. military, and is constantly found reading before shows. He teaches me about Ska, and Anarcho-punk music, and tells me to read Noam Chomsky and Smedley Butler. I don't think he and Van have ever discussed issues of race or social justice, otherwise a photo like this would be unlikely to exist. Had we been conscious of each other's politics, we never would have agreed to link arms and pose when one of our Korean friends suggested we get a shot "of just the American soldier punks."

That's me on the other end, in my faux-hawk, fist in the air. I'd love to tell you that I am as politically conscious, for better or for worse, as Ben and Van, but here in my mid-twenties I am ignorant and loud, sloppy and flirtatious. Like much of the skate punk I grew up listening to, I am brassy and angry, but only half-informed of any of the shit I talk about. There are certainly exceptions to this; I pay close attention to the lyrics of bands from my youth, as well as the new bands that I am introduced to from the international crowd of folks who gather in bars like Club Spot to get a taste of Korean Punk Rock. Though until I approached this scene, this weekend revelry in a college district of the city, I remain largely ignorant to the world going on around me. It takes this strange pack—the well-read sailor, the skinhead translator, a headstrong Jewish activist who refuses to return to the U.S.—to begin shaking my foundation. More than anything, it takes this music and the scene that surrounds it to begin my education.

It isn't serving and leading in the U.S. Army as we march to two wars that will eventually awaken me to caring about my part in the war racket. Nor is it starting college classes—later than most, while I am still serving—that will get me thinking about homophobia, colonialism, and environmental disaster. It's the music. I'm fully aware of how cliché the idea is, but it's fucking true; it has always been the music. It's the music for forgotten kids around the world whose schools are failing to teach them anything other than the myth of meritocracy and American exceptionalism. The Oppressed opened Van's eyes to police brutality and working-class unity (even if Skrewdriver filled him with racist, nationalistic pride). Rudimentary Pedi gave Ben the scaffolding to begin thinking about nihilism and the influence of popular media. It takes me a few years before I really get it, but the bands of my youth eventually teach me about our failure to sign the Kyoto Protocol, about toxic masculinity, and about the fact that millions resisted the tide of war that washed me up in uniform thousands of miles from home. It took the music to teach me that in their own small way—punk songs, marches, letters to President Bush, going to community college rather than joining the military—folks back home resisted while people like Van, Ben, and I let it overtake us, be it for pride, adventure, or escape from poverty.

It's a complicated photo, this shot of us. It isn't the military that unites us in any way; we tried to keep our service low-key when we were out in the clubs anyway. Maybe it's the scene, but even the scene couldn't ultimately repair our differences either. I can't imagine the three of us so much as talking to each other anymore. The shot isn't real unity at all, I guess, but it's a moment when—somewhere between simple cords and angry lyrics, between gulping down OB Lager and fried squid on the weekends tucked between long weeks of military uniforms and barracks life—music cast its spell on each of us.

MY SIDE OF THE FENCE

SOMEWHERE tucked into the Hongdae neighborhood of Seoul, a sweaty mass of teens and twenty-somethings is packed into a grungy basement venue. The mostly Korean crowd dresses in skate shoes, band tees, and buzzed hair. The room is tiny and dark; the walls and ceiling are lined with posters of long-past concerts. A small stage takes up a third of the room, and on nights like this, the crowd is shoulder to shoulder in the standing-room-only venue.

For the evening's headliner, the place is nearly overflowing. The band's biggest fans squeeze in toward the chest-level bar separating the stage from the crowd. The band's Korean lead singer takes the stage in a basketball jersey: a style popularized by hardcore punk bands of the American Midwest. Canadians, Australians, and Americans fill out the pack of outcast Korean youth and turn the mob into a capacity crowd.

Without warning or signal, the band launches into their first song of the night, one of many that blends both Korean and English lyrics. The crowd erupts. A group near the center is whipped into a swarm of jumping and kicking. Those of us near the front pump our fists and scream along with the verses.

As the anthem approaches, every hand in the room stabs skyward. The fists are Korean, and black and brown and white. They are stamped for admission. The young ones are backed with markered X's. The lead singer places his booted foot on the amplifier at the front of the stage and leans toward us as we shout, in unison, a single line.

"CHEONG-JU CITY HARDCORE."

For a moment, we are one.

This is everything that I had ever looked for in a social scene; everything I had wanted of the punk scene back in the U.S., but had missed by about a decade. We are a family of artists and politically minded kids who for some reason or another, spend each weekend bound together. We are exiles.

After the show, the crowd spills back out onto the street. The venue's entrance is located on a near-vertical alley ascending from a main thoroughfare of this Seoul neighborhood popular among college-aged outcasts and expatriates of all sorts. The scene remains friendly and excited, but the dynamic has changed just a bit.

"You don't see any, I don't know, conflicts of interest being a punk and being in the military?" a young Canadian teacher asks me in the cool evening air amid a group of Western expats.

English teachers are among one of the large group of foreigners living in Seoul: most are recently out of college and eager for a year or two of adventure overseas. Most are progressive folks. All of them are quick to distinguish themselves from the other large group of Westerners living in the city: American service members.

The scene is, at least superficially, welcoming. When military members find the small cluster of clubs that host punk rock shows in this neighborhood, they are generally welcomed, assuming that we behave ourselves. Most of us fit in nicely though; the soldiers who make the trip out here—rather than the quick trip to the foreign district, where drinks are expensive and company can be purchased cheaply—are here for a reason. We're progressives, or radicals, or nerds, or a combination of all three.

That is the real surprise though: not that U.S. soldiers rotate in and out of this scene, but that political, punk rock kids would join the army in the first place. I'm not the only one, but being a K-9 handler for the Military Police makes me an uncommon case.

To the young man challenging my presence, I should explain the connection between poverty and enlistment in the military. I should tell him that the same hardships that led me to punk rock are the ones that led me to escape from Reno. I should admit that I was naive and knew nothing of the military, so my profession in the military was decided very much at the whim of an army recruiter. I should say something about money for college. Of 9/11 knee-jerks.

"It's . . . complicated, I guess . . . ," I stutter out, beginning before I've formed a response.

"Lay off him, it's just a job," a feminine voice interrupts us. "I should ask you what business a kid who went to a private college has in a foreign punk scene." A round-faced young woman with her dark hair buzzed short and a handsome Jewish nose interrupts the Canadian man's response.

The woman's name is Unity. I have no idea what her real name is (I heard once maybe Laurie or Laura or Lauren); since being introduced a couple months ago, I've never heard her called anything but this. She teaches English too, although she doesn't come across as the professional type. She's wearing lace-up boots that are spray-painted pink and a bomber jacket with sloganed patches pinned all over. She has a great smile too.

Unity is bright. She is much more intelligent than I, but doesn't come across as snobbish. She isn't dumbing herself down for anyone, she just isn't a braggart. I listen closely when she speaks, not just because I recognize that she is smarter than me, but also because I have a bit of a crush on her. She has shown me around town in the weeks prior: introduced me to the hip record stores and her favorite street-art spots and a place where we can get soy ice cream. She makes sure to invite me to meet-ups that soldiers don't get invited to very often, and I make sure to come along and keep quiet. I am learning, slowly, how to be less insufferably conspicuous.

Her challenge to my inquisitor tonight is enough to end the awkward line of questioning; he drops the subject and moves on to another cluster of folks gathered on the narrow street. Unity and I continue talking, and the scene around us becomes a bit of a bazaar. We trade CDs and vinyl that are hard to find in shops around Seoul. We trade books that we've been discussing for weeks. We trade patches and stories and ideas. We share cans of Foster's beer, which the Koreans hate, the Americans love, and the Australians have never tasted.

"So did you hear about this protest next week?" Unity asks me from behind a chrome-colored beer can. "The one out near Pyeongtaek?"

I tell her that I had.

"We're going to be there, a group of us expats, sitting in with the local farmers." She's talking about a demonstration in the farm villages outside of Pyeongtaek where, for months, folks have been rallying in protest to the expansion of the nearby U.S. military base. The base is undergoing a rapid expansion to draw U.S. forces out of Seoul and into the more rural areas so as to reduce the visibility and social impact of the American military, a move which many progressive Koreans consider a consolation prize in lieu of their primary goal: getting the tens of thousands of U.S. soldiers who have occupied the peninsular nation since the 1950s out of Korea. The downside of this bargain is that a small farming village will be annexed and plowed over to make way for this expansion.

I know all this because I am stationed at this military base.

"I don't suppose that there is a chance you'll be joining us, huh?" She nudges me with her elbow and grins. She knows that I'm with her on a lot of issues, but that being a military member overseas, I'm restricted on what I can say or do politically. These kinds of conversations normally end with me wishing her and the rest of the crew well, but the mood is a bit more uncomfortable this time.

"I'm going to be working that day," I tell her, my face hiding nothing.

I don't have to say more. Looking at me with a hurt (and somehow sympathetic) stare, Unity understands the implication. She knows what I do for the military, what it means that I am working on a weekend. She knows what the army's working dogs are used for during protests. She doesn't know the acronym QRF, Quick Reaction Force, but she knows what the police response to a demonstration outside of a military base looks like. She understands immediately why my job isn't always *just a job*.

From my position, the protest is an awfully boring affair. Over the course of a weekend, I spend two ten-hour shifts in the front seat of a Korean SUV, listening to punk rock blare from headphones plugged into one ear, and listening to police radio traffic with the other. In the back seat rests Rollie, a 100-pound German shepherd in a large, plastic crate stenciled with DANGER, MILITARY WORKING DOG. His head rests on the floor of the crate, and he is looking up at me with big brown eyes whenever I glance back. Rollie sighs; he is bored.

"I hear ya, buddy."

The Korean National Police come out in enormous numbers for these types of events. Nearly every protest that I've witnessed outside of a military base hosts a human wall of Korean police that outnumber the demonstrators by nearly two-to-one. This is especially impressive during large protests, or protests of unknown numbers (like today) when several busloads worth of men in black jumpsuits and shoulder-high shields are transported in from around the region. This is a thoughtful bit on the part of U.S. and Korean authorities. These numbers are an effort taken to ensure that protestors rarely encounter U.S. military police forces during these events. Everyone from top commanders to the troops geared up with batons and shields know what kind of negative impact hands-on contact would have on international relations.

So we are hidden. In a parking lot far from the event, there are dozens of military police clad in riot gear; young men and women wearing helmets and masks and carrying batons and interlocking shields. They have been training in crowd control techniques all week, just in case something happens: in case someone breaks through. But we—both the troops in the gear and me, the guy with the dog—aren't a show of force; we are a contingency plan. We're in a lot a mile or so away from the side of the base that butts up against the village where the protests are organized. Down the road, there are Korean police with buses equipped to be used as barricades or bulldozers when needed. Beyond them, a 25-foot-tall, razor-wire-topped fence surrounds the base. Just outside the fence, several hundred more police with five-foot-long clubs stand shoulder-to-shoulder. There, just beyond the human wall of the national police, is a tiny farming community in its final days. On one side of the village is a dilapidated hovel, where Unity and a few other expats are working alongside hundreds of Koreans, helping to paint protest banners in English and doing interviews for any news outlets that ask.

I don't see any of this from my location. I see the interior of my Kia Santa Fe, and outside of my windshield, I see a handful of young military police, geared up, but resting on the asphalt in the parking lot where we wait, relieving their boredom by tossing pistachio shells at each other.

Life on the base proceeds as normal that weekend. The dining halls and the shopping center and the gym are all open for business. The liquor store is full and rapidly emptying. The embroidery shop is abuzz. The protests make international news every time they heat up, but other than a small travel advisory notifying folks leaving the military installation on foot of an ongoing demonstration, few troops other than the Military Police even take notice that day.

I have played in my head dozens of times the scenario where Unity and I meet eyes from opposing crowds during a storming of the base. An alternate history where I am forced to make decisions between duty and friendship, where the crowd is not placid, but angry and whipped into a frenzy. Unity at the head of a wave of Korean protestors as they fell a fence and swell over the levee of armored police. Rollie and I rush from our vehicle, my hand on his collar, and I order the crowd to freeze. Rollie is transformed into a snapping, snarling war machine at the end of my arm. Unity and I lock eyes and we both shake our heads as if to tell the other, don't do this. "MILITARY POLICE," I shout. "Halt, Halt, Halt or I'll release my dog. . . ."

This is fantasy though. On my side of the fence, the day is uneventful, and I am relieved. Unity will tell me later that she was proud of her work that weekend, although it is not so much as a speed bump when the time comes to raze the village and make way for expansion. In photos that I will later see of Unity, she looks teary-eyed, although I'm unsure whether it is because she believes that she can save the village, or because she knows it is doomed.

It is while driving home to my barracks room at the end of my shift that I see my first visual clue of anything out of the ordinary on base: a tattered red banner with a hand-painted message, affixed with plastic cable ties to the perimeter fence.

"Go Home."

*

This is not where Unity and I part ways, although I regret to say that we do, in fact, part ways. It happens in a tiny apartment in one of the many unremarkably boxy high-rise buildings in the suburbs of Seoul. Although I am a bit too intimidated by Unity to ever make a move, she has no such objection and asks me if I'd like to come over for dinner.

Most of the evening is agreeable and quaint: we order-in from a place that she is convinced is at least vegetarian, if not vegan. We sit on the hardwood floor of her tiny apartment and listen to American and British punk albums and we talk about Seoul and home and the scene and anything but politics. She invites me to stay the night, which I do. I get the impression she is hoping that I will make a move, but—as my brothers in uniform tell me—I "lack closing skills." We wind up cuddling in her bed, nothing more. Tonight she is uncharacteristically docile, and as we lie in the dark, she rests her head on my bare chest as I stare at the ceiling.

In bed we are close, close enough to discuss what had occurred a few weeks prior.

"It's wild what happened, us being on opposite sides of the fence and all," she says, breaking the silence.

"It really is. I hate these sorts of things, but I suppose that I understand both sides of the argument."

"You what?" she says as she lifts her head to look me in the eyes.

"I get both sides: the plight of these people and why they'd be mad, but also the need for relocating forces outside of Seoul."

"The U.S. is an occupying force stealing the ancestral home of these farmers!" she snaps, glaring at me with harsh, skeptic eyes.

"We are . . . The U.S. is here as a guest of the Korean people," I reply. (A standard talking point given to U.S. forces serving in Korea.) "The move is important to the future rela-

tions between the Korean government and the U.S. military."
(Another.)

"Why exactly do you think that the U.S. is even here in
the first place? What justifies them staying?"

"I don't know. I guess . . . we came here to defend South
Korea during the war, and we've stayed as a deterrent
against invading forces."

"The goal is reunification, not invasion, you know that.
Besides, you don't think that the U.S. having a footprint in
mainland Asia plays a big part of it?"

"Only incidentally. We are here as allies to Korean people. In many cases, among those old enough to remember the
war, we're welcomed as guests here."

We recede into silence. The room remains quiet long
enough for things to feel uncomfortable: silent enough and
still enough that we begin to recognize the difference between
our upbringings, our educational backgrounds, our current
stations in life. When I recall this conversation years later, it
is filed under "naivety." It will be a while before I start understanding how right she is about all of this, about most of the
things she said to me during our time together.

"Tony," she begins, shaking her head with disappointment.
"I think that you and I just come from different worlds." It
is the last thing she tells me before returning her head to my
chest, closing her eyes, and resting.

PAGEANT

IMAGINE A SOLDIER.

What do you see?

Is it a man? Is he white? Maybe a clean, young face and a close haircut. Maybe a rough, old leatherface, cigarette hanging out of his mouth. Maybe it's *Platoon* you see. Maybe it's *M*A*S*H**. Maybe you see a sibling who served. A son. An uncle. If a war has ripped its way into your home, maybe it's not a soldier at all, but a box and a flag.

Imagine a soldier.

I never know what to say when people tell me that I don't look like I served in the army. They're right. I don't, but I have a hard time putting together what is meant by this. I'd like to think they mean beard, but I've met plenty of veterans who are successfully wearing the lumberjack look. I'd like to think that when people tell me that I don't look like a soldier, they mean "you've got a bit of a tummy," or even "you look like a hipster." I'd prefer not to think that they mean "I hear your lisp. I see your *swish.*"

Imagine a soldier.

What is he doing? Is he holding a rifle? Is he hiking, with a heavy pack weighing him down? Posing with Iraqi youth, offering a camera the two-finger sign for peace? What is it that soldiers do during the day? When they aren't in combat. When they aren't training. What goes on in the toybox when our nation isn't playing war?

Here's a picture of a soldier. In a bar, two middle-aged men with scruff on their faces and paint on their jeans slam oversized tokens onto the counter of their local VFW post. They laugh, sharing stories and can after can after can. The tokens are challenge coins, weighty discs etched with the logos and slogans of military units. The men received the coins for merit: informal awards from military commanders for something outstanding: not a life-saving sort of event though, that would warrant a ribbon or medal. No, the act had to be something more routine. A well-executed inspection. Zero accidents in X days. The men sling their coins onto the bar, telling a story about it, where they received it, who it's from. It's customary that the soldier with the coins from the person with the least prestigious background buys the rest a round of drinks.

This is fiction. The whole scene. I've never stepped foot in a VFW hall. I've never thrown a coin down on any bar. My coins are in a sandwich bag in a cardboard box in a storage closet. I don't know anyone who has actually bought a drink or been bought a drink like this. The whole ritual is something told from one soldier to another, but always spoken, never performed.

Here's a picture of a soldier. I received my pile of coins by means of the Soldier of the Year competition. A pageant, or at least something near what you might imagine a pageant to look like. During my sixth year in the army, my bosses identified me as a particularly strong candidate for a competition meant to identify exceptional performers in the army. Not exceptional at soldiering as you might picture it: running, shooting, following orders. I was good at performing, like a young woman with a sash on a stage. At the higher levels of the competition, some more functional tasks were brought in: land navigation, assembling and disassembling weapons, commanding a squad through a mock Iraqi village, but for most of the circuit, we were pageant contestants.

Each month, soldiers selected by their unit would meet on military bases in one of the more civically purposed buildings (offices, libraries, meeting halls). We'd don our best dress uniforms: our brass polished; our green suits cleaned and pressed; our hair clipped, fresh from the barber's chair. The women's hair would be pulled tightly back into headache-inducing buns. We waited for the review board, a panel of the base's military leadership who, in addition to judging our appearance and the subjective category of *military bearing,* would drill us on the various aspects of military knowledge, firing off one obscure question after the other.

These competitions turned the back offices of these buildings into the backstage at convention centers and suburban hotels where Little Miss Townsville pageants take place across the country. Every soldier would take a different approach to backstage. Some would primp, lint-rolling their coat for the twentieth time, or constantly adjusting their gigline, the line formed by aligning the shirt, belt buckle and pant crotch uniformly. Others paced while quizzing themselves before the board.

"Sergeant Major, the deadliest war in American history was the Civil War."

"Sergeant Major, the image appearing on the Medal of Honor is that of Minerva, the goddess of righteous war."

"Sergeant Major, as of today, the toll in Afghanistan is . . ."

Others would sit around with pageant veterans, sharing tips and wearing the cool cloak of experience.

"Did you check current events today? You gotta check the morning's news before these things."

"I'm glad Gunny Thomas isn't sitting on the board this time; his questions are the worst."

"Last month I would have taken it, but my slacks had hanger creases across them."

When our time came, the whole event rolled out like a recital. The question, review, and evening gown portions came all at once. Knock three times exactly, not too softly, but not too forcefully either. Close the door behind you; don't slam it. Offer the salute and report. Hold the salute until returned. Perform the facing and marching movements in front of them crisply; practice in a mirror beforehand. Practice in your low-quarter shoes on carpet. As they judge your movement and appearance, don't look at them; stare straight ahead. Take your seat only when told to do so. Begin or end each response with the judge's rank. Yes, Sergeant Major. No, Sergeant Major. I don't have an answer to that question at this time, Sergeant Major. Respond with complete sentences. Respond confidently, even if you're wrong. When dismissed, be sure to salute again. Leave the room in the most direct route. Close the door behind you; don't slam it. Don't talk about the questions with the other contestants.

Imagine a soldier.

It's being queer that brought me to these competitions. It was the opportunity to excel and to know that in an army that demanded its queer soldiers to lie about their identity, we were thriving. Granted, I don't know whether I would have had the guts to come out, even if I had won at the top level, U.S. Army Soldier of the Year (our Miss America). Still, part of me hoped that I could have been a secret whispered among queer troops. A queer army icon. Representation inside of silence. What gets beneath my skin about being told that I don't look like a soldier is that I worry it means that bookish, queer boys can't cut it there. That is why I competed.

Imagine a soldier.

Perhaps my offense comes from the flatness of the image of the soldier too. That mainstream perception doesn't include the young, educated Indian who joined the U.S. Army to become a citizen, or the twenty-something professional who joined to find a way to pay for his wife's medical care. It certainly doesn't include the working-class queer who came out for his teen years before being pushed back in to fit an army mold. It upsets me because soldiers are a spectrum, many faces and individual identities molded into cogs for the machine. Maybe underneath it all, I'm upset because we are a nation at war, and the lack of understanding is another demonstration of low investment, the lack of skin in the game. Or maybe I'm embarrassed because of how little skin I had in the game.

Imagine a soldier.

"Where did you serve?" It's a question veterans often hear, both from other vets and from those who have not served. Like "where are you from?" it's a question that can mean a lot of things. Which military base were you stationed at? What unit were you in? Though, most often, the question is meant as an inquiry into war-time service. Iraq or Afghanistan? Which forward operating base?

I never went to war.

I joined the army in the wake of September 11th. I spent eight years serving during a period of two wars. I spent almost five years of that time working with an explosive detector dog, a task desperately needed in the contemporary theaters of war. I never went. If I were a religious or spiritual person, I would say, "It wasn't in the cards." I would say, "God has other plans for me." But I'm not either of those things. I just say I never went. I'd like to say that I don't feel any guilt about this situation. That I felt proud of the work I did elsewhere, and that that was enough. After all, it wasn't all smiling, posing, and answering questions. But the truth is, I have mixed feelings about *not going*. Some guilt. Some relief. A morbid part of me I am not supposed to acknowledge wishes I had a war story for you, and part of me is afraid to consider what could have happened out there, me walking in front of a convoy of military vehicles, with a dog and a leash and a Kevlar vest and hope. Honestly, I don't want to shoot at another human any more than I want a human shooting at me. There's a sense of bullets dodged, but there's also a sense of guilt for lives lost. Call it not-quite-survivor-guilt, but witness guilt.

In October of 2008, I was named Noncommissioned Officer of the Year for my military base. After several levels of competition and months of training, I looked the best, had the best-crafted biographical sketch, wrote the best essay, and answered the most useless questions. My commander patted me on the back. Round after round of my peers and supervisors congratulated me on my hard work. I received hundreds of dollars in checks. Liberty Bonds. Reserved parking spaces around base. No sash, but dozens of challenge coins from local military leaders.

When a challenge coin is presented, it is done so with a handshake.

"Great job, Sergeant." The coin is slipped from one hand to the next, often awkwardly, as both participants maintain eye contact the whole time. "You deserve this."

I don't remember saying it now, but the on-base newspaper interviewed me the day I received the honor. About the review board, I was quoted:

"It's intimidating at first," Moll said. "It's a high-stress situation."

That month Al Qaeda commander Mahir al-Zubaydi is killed by U.S. troops. AFRICOM, a new U.S. military command created for the purported purpose of responding to threats of terrorism in Africa, is activated in Stuttgart, Germany. U.S. Commanders of NATO request increased authority in pursuing drug-related crimes in Afghanistan.

In October of 2008, the news stations boasted that U.S. forces had sustained the lowest amount of combat deaths in four years. Only thirty service members were killed in Iraq and Afghanistan that month. Only thirty. Thirty volunteers. Thirty Families. Thirty. Thirty. Thirty. *"It's a high-stress situation."* Thirty. Only. Daniel Wallace. Scott Metcalf. Bradley Coleman. Nicholas Casey. Thirty. SSG Grieco. Capt. Yurista. PFC Egglestone. SSG Hause. CPL Robles. Thirty Families. Sim. Taylor. Lindenau. Dryden. Borjas. Penich. Pickard. *"It's intimidating at first."* Bertrand. Fortunato. Saint. McCraw. Medley. Dimond. Johnson. *The installation recognized some of its finest Soldiers in a ceremony Friday at garrison head-quarters.* Reuben Fernandez III. Jason Karella. Michael Clark. William Rudd. Michael Stahlman. Tavarus Setzler. Jason E. von Zerneck.

Imagine a soldier.

What do you see?

CASUALTIES

SOMEWHERE in this book I should mention the number of lives, both military and civilian, both coalition and local, that the wars in Iraq and Afghanistan ended. Somewhere in this book I should mention the number of lives, both military and civilian, both coalition and local, that the wars in Iraq and Afghanistan ended. Somewhere in this book I should mention the number of lives, both military and civilian, both coalition and local, that the wars in Iraq and Afghanistan ended. Somewhere in this book I should mention the number of lives, both military and civilian, both coalition and local, that the wars in Iraq and Afghanistan ended. Somewhere in this book I should mention the number of lives, both military and civilian, both coalition and local, that the wars in Iraq and Afghanistan ended. Somewhere in this book I should mention the number of lives, both military and civilian, both coalition and local, that the wars in Iraq and Afghanistan ended. Somewhere in this book I should mention the number of lives, both military and civilian, both coalition and local, that the wars in Iraq and Afghanistan ended. Somewhere in this book I should mention the number of lives, both military and civilian, both coalition and local, that the wars in Iraq and Afghanistan ended. Somewhere in this book I should mention the number of lives, both military and civilian, both coalition and local, that the wars in Iraq and Afghanistan ended. Somewhere in this book I should mention the number of lives, both military and civilian, both coalition and local, that the wars in Iraq and Afghanistan ended. Somewhere in this book I should mention the number of lives, both military and civilian, both coalition and local, that the wars in Iraq and Afghanistan ended. Somewhere in this book I should mention the number of lives, both military and civilian, both coalition and local, that the wars in Iraq and Afghanistan ended. Somewhere in this book I should mention the number of lives, both military and civilian, both coalition and local, that the wars in Iraq and Afghanistan ended. Somewhere in this book I should mention the number of lives, both military and civilian, both coalition and local, that the wars in Iraq and Afghanistan ended. Somewhere in this book I should mention the number of lives, both military and civilian, both coalition and local, that the wars in Iraq and Afghanistan ended. Somewhere in this book I should mention the number of lives, both military and civilian, both coalition and local, that the wars in Iraq and Afghanistan ended. Somewhere in this book I should mention the number of lives, both military and civilian, both coalition and local, that the wars in Iraq and Afghanistan ended. Somewhere in this book I should mention the number of lives, both military and civilian, both coalition and local, that the wars in Iraq and Afghanistan ended. Somewhere in this book I should mention the number of lives, both military and civilian, both coalition and local, that the wars in Iraq and Afghanistan ended. Somewhere in this book I should mention the number of lives, both military and civilian, both coalition and local, that the wars in Iraq and Afghanistan ended. Somewhere in this book I should mention the number of lives, both military and civilian, both coalition and local, that the wars in Iraq and Afghanistan ended. Somewhere in this book I should mention the number of lives, both military and civilian, both coalition and local, that the wars in Iraq and Afghanistan ended. Somewhere in this book I should mention the number of lives, both military and civilian, both coalition and local, that the wars in Iraq and Afghanistan ended.

PHOTO: SLICK SLEEVES

HERE, with my uniform recently dry-cleaned, my brass recently shined, my hair closely cut, and my staff sergeant insignia newly sewn onto the uniform, I am just beginning to wake up to how I feel about my military service. This one, seven years in, will be my last official military photo, but I still remember my first.

The first official uniform photo that soldiers have taken is shot before they even begin their basic training experience. In the in-processing battalion, in the building on training installations where new enlistees are shipped and stored for several days before they begin their training, we are inventoried as new resources of the U.S. government. Our paperwork is processed, we are given our first (long) series of immunizations, and we are stripped of the adornments that make us individual people. The men are given sixty-second haircuts down to the scalp, and we are all walked through a supply line where we are fitted ("Size, recruit?") and issued our first uniforms. Just after the haircut and general issue, we are cycled through a line in which we (terrified, confused, full of fear and those recent injections) have a photo taken in our dress green jackets in front of the Stars and Stripes.

This is the photo that is sent to mothers, fathers, boyfriends and girlfriends, the photo that goes in our basic training yearbook (seriously), and the first real documentation of our conversion into soldiers.

For many who don't make military service a career, for those who do a brief stint for college money or to escape their provincial life, this will be the only official military photo they have taken. This is also true for many of those who will be slain before they take another photo. Because I was bored, and proud, and stubborn enough to engage with the army's Non-commissioned Officer of the Year competition, and because I was being groomed for a long career in the military, my first sergeant asked me to take another official photo, seven years after my chubby-faced, wide-eyed, in-processing picture at Fort Leonard Wood, Missouri, one to hang in the base head-quarters and dining halls of our military installation.

The uniform I am wearing in the later photo is a suit made of dark green wool and polyester. Officially, the color is designated by the government as "shade 44," and it is a change from the olive drab uniform that it replaced in 1954 when the color became so popular that the army worried its colors were being "debased." My suit has a black name-plate affixed to one pocket, and marksman badges for several firearms affixed to the other. Several rows of ribbons are attached just over the badges, a rainbow of colors that designate my accomplishments during military service. Civilians tend to assume this means I have seen a lot of wartime conflict, but the truth is that not a one of them is for fighting or deploying to war, a fact made evident by my slick sleeves.

Used as a singular noun, a "slick sleeve" is a person, usually of some rank, who has no combat patch on the right sleeve of their uniform, the decoration that distinguishes which unit a soldier deployed to combat with. In the first decade of the new millennium, when repeat and lengthy deployments to the two wars in which the U.S. had found itself entrenched, the term grew in popularity as a pejorative thrown by those who had gone to war, men and women who assumed that, with such a robust operating tempo, a "slick sleeve" must be pulling strings in order to dodge deployment orders.

That's the paradox of combat service. Few people enjoy being away from their family for twelve to sixteen months, in the snow-flecked mountains of Afghanistan or the blistering deserts of Iraq, being constantly under the threat of mortar attacks, but one feels an obligation to *do one's part,* as well as a resentment for those who lack this feeling of obligation. Go to war, hate it, complain about it, but never dodge the threat.

I am a "slick sleeve," and when soldiers see a staff sergeant in the highly deployable job of training and handling explosive-detecting dogs, they are convinced that I must be dodging my trip "over there." The truth is, even though I selected this assignment close to the nation's capital because I was promised the adventure of protecting the president and other VIPs, I would be lying if I didn't say that I selected it over military bases that were significantly more likely to deploy.

I'm not particularly eager to fight, kill, or die, and this photo was taken around the time that I figured that all out. At the start of 2009, seven and a half years after the start of the war in Afghanistan, and nearly six years into the war in Iraq, my ability to rationalize the contradictory beliefs of my politics and my continued military service has grown thin. The look on my face in this photo, it is severe, and it's complicated. In part, I feel the pressure of phrases like "slick sleeve," and in part, I cannot escape the effects of a culture of hypermasculinity, but behind all that, it is growing more difficult to accommodate my uniform, my stripes, my title as the base's Noncommissioned Officer of the Year, with what has happened, what is happening, what is likely to happen, when the U.S. military *visits* a nation.

What is beneath the sleeves marks the sort of person I am becoming. Beneath the uniform are my new tattoos, one, a pistol to represent my desire never to fire a weapon again, another, the image of a tank being smashed by a wrench.

Hiding on my body, beneath the uniform that signifies who I am, are the marks of who I want to be—a resister, a peacenik.

The photo is a shot of me caught between two spaces, a contradiction. Here I am an expert marksman who is happy that he has never gone to war, a rising military leader who stopped believing in the U.S. military's role in the world. Here I have stopped believing in the narrative that has been offered to me for the last seven years, and I have yet to fully uncover who exactly I will become once I finally take off my uniform and put it away for the last time.

DOGS OF WAR

"What did you do in the Army?" a student asks me before class, her dreads rolling over the hand propping up her face. Or a colleague over drinks in a dive bar. Or a professional in a dress shirt and tie, interviewing me for a job that has nothing to do with the army. I get the impression that folks are unsure if they are supposed to ask this. There is a hesitancy in the utterance that suggests that a lot of people are told not to ask vets about their time in the military anymore. There's a feeling hidden there, just below the surface, something that I've yet to pin down, something to do with fear of offending, something to do with guilt.

I used to say *Military Working Dog Handler,* but something about the double adjective, double noun caused heads to cock as they interpreted what I meant.

I said *K-9 handler* for a while too, as an intentional shortening of the title, but saying *K-9* instead of *dog* sounded a bit like jargon. On top of that, I always thought the term invoked images of vicious attack dogs. Sure, our dogs were that, but it wasn't the body of what we did, and it wasn't the image I wanted associated with my service. Part of me wants to avoid associating my service with law enforcement altogether. Growing up poor, I never really liked cops. Cops never seemed to be on the side of my family, a perspective amplified by a college education that offered me a glimpse of some of the ugly history of police in the U.S., particularly those with dogs: hunting slaves, attacking civil rights marchers, beating queer people in our nightclubs and outing us to the press. Like my military service, doing police work is something I am still trying to reconcile with my ethics.

Lately I've been saying *bomb-sniffing dog handler,* which is wordy again, but which suggests something other than snapping police dogs. *Bomb* gets people's attention right away, and when paired with *dog,* the title seems to be words that those around me are familiar with hearing together. People love dogs and hate bombs. I want to be able to define my service in a way that is difficult for people to dislike—both other people and myself.

2008—U.S. Occupied Iraq

"Cute little puppy, huh?" the video begins, with the sound of desert wind whipping around the camera's microphone. The Marine is in full gear—armored vest, helmet, goggles, likely burdened with a full combat load—between 97 to 135 pounds of gear, armor, ammunition, and weapons—Full Battle Rattle.

He is gripping this *cute little puppy* by the nape of the neck; it dangles in his gloved hands expressionless, vacant. He stands at the edge of a desert cliff, midday.

"Awwww, so cute," a second Marine, the one holding the camera, states as he leans into the shot.

The Marine cocks the arm clasping the puppy rearward, something close to how we soldiers learn to throw a grenade. Something resembling a hook shot. The camera follows the launch, watching the mass tumble through the air and downward into the canyon.

"That was mean, Motari," the second Marine jokes as he chuckles.

Back on the homefront, the public conversations that follow the video are varied. As a nation, we discuss the mental strain on service members caused by repeated, prolonged deployments to combat zones. We discuss whether or not there is a continued need for combat troops in Iraq five years after the start of the war, four years and ten months after Bush's Mission Accomplished, just over a year into *the surge*. We say *traumatic stress* and *coping mechanism,* or instead, *a few bad apples*. Some ask if the video is real. Some suggest that the puppy was already dead, that the Marine hurled a corpse off the cliff and that the yelping was a post-production effect.

In my office, back in the States, the Military Working Dog team of the 241st Military Police detachment, we say, *What an asshole. His career is over. I can't believe they posted that on the Internet. If I ever got a hold of that dude . . .*

2009—Fort Myer, VA
Danyel finishes her story with a laugh.

"So, this lady is like, 'I can't believe people would do that to dogs, turn them into bombs.'"

We laugh. Stupid civilians. The lady has misunderstood what is meant by bomb dog. *Who could do such a thing?* is the question on our minds. *Who could believe that their military is capable of that type of cruelty?* None of the dog handlers there that day are old enough to remember that during WWII, Soviet soldiers strapped dogs with explosives and trained them to run beneath German tanks. Initially, these explosives were set with timers, but the task of estimating time became dangerous, particularly when the dogs would run to the tanks, and then return to the handler for their reward, bringing with them the ticking bomb. This was resolved by changing the device to explode on contact, often with an antenna that, when broken, say, by the edge of a tank as the dog crawled beneath it, would detonate the device.

2005—Army Publishing Directorate, VA

The U.S. Army keeps track of how-tos and best practices in field manuals, unclassified booklets containing a mix of technical jargon and inspirational rhetoric. The 2005 update of Army Field Manual 3–19.17, Military Working Dogs, suggests the following:

> The highly aggressive dog tactics of the 1960s and 1970s are long gone. Today's MWD program effectively employs expertly trained and motivated handlers coupled with highly intelligent breeds of dogs. These teams are continuously rotating between their assigned duties and deployments worldwide to perform joint operations, multiechelon tasks, and interagency missions.

2008—Fort Meade, MD

"You, in the field," I begin again. "I'm Sergeant Moll with the Military Police. I'm accompanied by a Military Working Dog. I'd like you to come and talk with me."

We call the man in the field a decoy. He's filling in for an actual bad guy, or at least, a twenty-five-year-old soldier's perception of a bad guy. He's waddling back and forth erratically, his movement limited by the padded, jute protective suit. He's the person getting bit today.

"Halt, Halt, Halt or I'll release my dog!"

The leash is dropped. The hound dashes toward the bite. 42 teeth. 320 pounds of pressure.

This is how the military trains. Rote memorization. Ritual. Muscle memory, the idea that one trains in a task until it has lost meaning, until it is reflex, so that it can be accomplished even when you've reached mental exhaustion. I've repeated this task a thousand times, always the same words, the same moves.

Catching the bad guys is not our primary mission. Our main job is to find bombs. Our job is to walk around pointing to places where the dog should put its nose, or to let it search on its own at the end of a leash. Working just outside of D.C. means the opportunity to protect the President, the Vice President and their families. It means long hours most days, but it also means bragging in bars. This sounds glamorous, but it also involves a constant routine of picking up dog shit, of wearing fur and slobber all over our uniforms, and of constantly smelling damp and rank.

It *feels* glamorous though, at least to us it does. My comrades and I show up at places in trucks marked *K-9*. We strut into anywhere we wish with German Shepherds and Belgian Malinois at our sides.

"Best job in the Army," we tell folks, smiling and kneeling down to pet the dog.

This too is how the military trains.

This is how they get twenty-somethings to do outlandish things, by telling them that they are superheroes. By giving them authority and telling them that they're fighting the good fight. This is where responsibility gets lost.

2004—U.S. Occupied Abu Ghraib

In the photograph, the one that made its rounds, a man is clad in an orange jumpsuit, on his knees, with his hands behind his back, restrained. His eyes are opened wide and staring into the eyes of a black Dutch shepherd that stands, unmuzzled and panting, inches from his face. The man's mouth looks as though his teeth are clenched, as though he has been pleading or crying. The dog has the man cornered into the makeshift wooden walls of the prison we've come to call Abu Ghraib. Behind the dog, holding the leash, is a man dressed in desert-patterned fatigues, with a woodland-colored armored vest, straddling the dog and staring at the man on his knees. This has become the image associated with the use of working dogs to torture detained humans at the U.S. Army-ran prison facility just west of Baghdad. I imagine that this image was shown more than the others due to censorship, both prude and patriotic, because our televi-

sion stations could not show the photos of the dogs gnash-
ing toward a nude man, a bound figure standing with his
penis tucked between his thighs and with his knees clasped
together to protect his genitals from being ripped from his
body.

Public schools don't teach poor kids about the ugly role
U.S. soldiers have played in American history. We learn about
the greatest generation, about the liberation of concentration
camps. We don't learn about the soldiers guarding our own
concentration camps during the same time, when over a hundred thousand Japanese-Americans were pulled from their
lives and sent to wartime camps. We weren't taught about the
soldiers at Kent State, at the Ludlow Massacre, at Wounded
Knee. The same can be said about the anti-war movement. We
learned about hate-filled hippies spitting on returning draft-
ees, and not about the well-reasoned international efforts to
resist each imperial march to war. We watch *Star Wars,* never
believing that the U.S. could be the empire. It isn't that Abu
Ghraib or Kent State define the American soldier; it's that we
children of the plebs are rarely offered the complete picture.
The sort of kids who go on to pledge their lives to military
service never hear about American failure until it is too late.

Famed psychologist Philip Zimbardo has spent his life
attempting to uncover what makes humans act evil. Examin-
ing instances like Abu Ghraib, the architect of the Stanford
Prison Experiment suggests that when people ask *How could
this have happened?* we should first consider three questions:
*What do people bring into the situation? What does the situ-
ation bring out of them? What is the system that creates and
maintains this situation?*

In other words, what does the line between bad apple
and rotten barrel look like?

2005—Fort Irwin, CA

"And what if they don't listen to your commands?"

"We give them a slight correction."

"What do you mean a *slight correction*?"

"A sharp verbal correction paired with a slight physical stimulation at their choke chain."

I've gotten good at this, using the euphemistic, sanitized language of the military. I don't yet realize how gross it is, because at this age, somewhere near the middle of my military experience, sometime in my early twenties, I believe it. At this point, I'm a company man.

I call Mary, an old flame, to flirt, to brag about how well I think I am doing. Mary is less impressed than I imagined at the job I am performing in the military.

"So you choke them?"

"No, this is just a sharp jerk on their leash. We only choke them when they refuse to release something from their mouth, when they won't release a bite on a bad guy or won't give their toy reward back. It's called escape avoidance."

"Oh. That is much better," she replies sarcastically.

"This is a serious business. I love my dog, but it is essential that they are trained to precision." I am sure, at some point in this conversation, that I say the words *Life and Death* to express graveness. I am sure I say *classic conditioning* to borrow authority.

"I can't imagine what you would do if they did something serious. Like, what would happen if they bit someone they weren't supposed to, or if they bit you?"

"We helicopter them."

"Helicopter?"

Helicopter, as one might imagine, is not a term appearing in any training manual. It isn't something endorsed anywhere, not explicitly. It is a technique handlers are told, when no one is looking, to use in extreme cases, and even then, only when no one is looking.

"We spin them around in circles several times at the end of their choke chain, and then use the momentum to thrust them to the ground. When they hit the ground, we bark a command at them. It disorients the dog and gets them refocused." (I don't say *hard reset.*)

"Christ, Tony. I can't believe you would do something so cruel. Do you hear yourself?"

"These aren't pets, Mary. These are war dogs. We do what it takes to get the mission done."

2009—Fort Meade, MD

The cancer has already spread when they find the lump. The dog has been acting lethargic, and when his handler recognizes it, he rushes him to the veterinarians on base.

The U.S. military classifies its working dogs as equipment. This categorization is made for the sake of keeping track of dogs that are deployed globally, and so that units can quickly replace one once it has reached the end of its service. Dog, Patrol/Explosives Detection, Line Item Number S33742; National Stock Number 8820-00-188-3880. *It is not necessary to wait until an MWD dies or becomes incapacitated to requisition a replacement.*

We call Junior our mascot. The long-haired German Shepherd is gentle enough for kids to pet in public, and has placed well in every competition he has ever entered. Despite rules stating otherwise, Junior's handler often allows him to cuddle up on the office couch during downtime, and none of us are ever bothered to object to it. Junior has been requested by name for VIP missions with the Secret Service—he has even helped to protect the Pope. His one weakness, the one thing that undermines his years of training, is the sight of a squirrel. But then, he is a dog.

Our whole squad is called when they made the decision to euthanize. That afternoon, in the recovery room of the vet's office, where they keep the chew toys and the Milk Bones, a beefy Puerto Rican from Jersey who works with Junior holds our mascot's head in his lap and runs his hands through the long hair. Four more of us, all in uniform, kneel beside the team as the vet gives the injection. None of us do a good job hiding our tears from each other. The youngest member of our squad lifts the top of his undershirt from beneath his coat and wipes the snot and tears from his face. The boss is standing with his arms crossed and his head hung, trying to sniffle his tears back into his face. I sit, knees bent, on the linoleum floor shaking my head, sucking in my lower lip as I sob.

PHOTO: DRESSED UP

THE PHOTO you don't see, the one that I only show Internet strangers and the queerest, closest friends, is the one that damns the narrative. It is some variant of the photo that each of you have hiding somewhere: your blue-collar husband on his knees with a collar and leash. Your ex-girlfriend in front of a bathroom mirror, a photo in a secret folder on your laptop, or in an old email inbox your wife doesn't know about. Or it is the photo of yourself, the one where your abs looked their best after a workout and a shower, or the dressing room shot of the lingerie that fits you perfectly.

The lingerie fits me perfectly. With a body still tight from the army, my thighs show off between the panties and thigh-high stockings. The tartan red dress is hiked high enough that you can see both. My makeup isn't flawless, but it is as close as one could get using supermarket cosmetics and You-Tube tutorials. Still, the look feels convincing enough that men flirt with me online. If you haven't been to those corners of the Internet lately, there are always men who want to flirt with people of any sex or gender dressed up pretty.

I'm dressed up pretty: patent leather heels, a Jennifer Aniston wig with blonde highlights. My nails are recently done.

I'm not model pretty, but with a nice tan and dressed up to tease, I'm at least Hot Topic pretty, trying-too-hard-at-the-mall pretty.

You want to say *transgender*, because that is something you've learned a lot about in the last few years. You know all about Laverne Cox and Laura Jane Grace, so you want to say *transition* or *gender identity*. Or maybe you're a quick study, no way this queer writer is going to get one over on you. You're going to say *drag*—exaggerated beauty, performance. You want to guess that I'm dressed to entertain, and in a sense you're right.

I'm dressed to have sex. If not in person, then online, Skyping as some complete stranger tells me what he wants me to do.

The photo remains unshared because it muddles two narratives. First, straight folk want clear lines drawn around their understanding of sex and gender. I'm not transgender—I'm not living as a woman, and I don't plan on transitioning. Nor am I a drag performer—though I have this look mastered at this point, you won't catch me out in public dressed up, and certainly not on a stage. If you've been reading queer literature closely enough, strange poems and prose from bears and queers, faggots and sissies, maybe you've caught the shape of things. Whether we're experimenting in our mother's clothes, or getting dolled up for Johns or our husbands, some queer men dress up in ways that aren't permitted. Most straight folks don't get to see these photos very often because they're still arguing with their cousins about Caitlyn Jenner while we're living enormously, containing multitudes.

But then again, it's often straight men I'm showing off for. I'm showing off with half-hearted caution though—the photo is cropped to show just a quarter of my face in bright lipstick and dark eyeshadow, a measure I hope is enough to keep me from being outed as some strange man unworthy of running for office or teaching your college students someday down the road.

The other story that gets fucked up is the narrative of gay and lesbian soldiers who are "just like you." Here in the first months of my transition out of the military, when I go from warrior to advocate working to remove the policy that keeps queer folks from serving openly, I'm repeating the talking point that "we're just like you." In blog posts and letters to elected officials, all of us advocates keep telling America how "just like you" we are. We want the same things that you do: service to our country, a family and a home in the suburbs, finding the one person we love and entering into a lifelong religious and legal union with that one person. All of that gets queered when you see a recent veteran dressed in heels, lying back on his checkered comforter, one hand frozen in action of slipping the dress up just a little bit more. It gets blurry when you hear that my girlfriend at the time snapped the photo for me, that she is one of a handful of women who get to see me like this. Swapping flag-waving one day for heels and makeup the next doesn't fit into any of that—it fits better with the fact that there is a whole queer reality just under the surface, just beneath the battle-dress uniform, beneath the flag, beneath the suburbs, barely hidden behind everything you want to call America.

LAST YEAR

ON DECEMBER 21, 2009, just shy of eight years after I left home in a hurry to join the U.S. Army, I am in the driver's seat, leaving an army base in suburban Maryland, wearing my uniform for the last time.

"I know you're not going to miss it," my first sergeant, a refrigerator of a man in army fatigues, told me just before I left. "A lot of guys do, but you've got some things going for you." It's one of the last things said to me in uniform, offered just before I step out into the winter air. This is my final commendation from a military leader.

On December 22, 2010, just a year after my last day in the army, the world's most powerful man pulls back a wooden chair and sits down at a desk on a stage decorated with the flags of each branch of service. The President is in a dark suit. A small American flag pin rests on his lapel. Behind him is a small crowd of lawmakers also in dark suits, except for the women in bright colors, huddling in to be seen by the cameras. The Chairman of the military's Joint Chiefs of Staff neither smiles nor frowns as he stands in his Navy dress uniform. The Vice President grins his old man grin. The two former service members on stage are at the end of a tour of duty in which they have acted as the face of a law that said that those who love members of the same sex were unfit to serve openly in the military.

The President, smiling, signs the paper on the desk, a bill transforms into law. They call it a repeal. We call it wrong made right. He signs it with two boxes full of pens, a strange standard applied whenever new laws are signed, and when he is finished, he looks out at the crowd, smiling. He slaps his palm down at the table. "This is done."

In December 2009, I don't come out of the closet. I should say, I don't come *back* out of the closet. I was out at sixteen, but the aforementioned law pushed me into this strange sort of bullshitting for eight years in which many people seemed to assume I was queer, but in which I wasn't allowed to say it. Or to hold hands. Or to go on dates anywhere near the bases where I was stationed. Or to visit the barracks rooms of other queer soldiers without the heart-thudding fear of being burst in on. I don't come back out for two more months, despite being hired by the biggest gay and lesbian nonprofit organization in the country. I'm on separation leave, leave time spent at the end of my contract for the sake of making my last day of work arrive a few weeks earlier. This means that although I'm out of the army, I'm still, technically, in the army on paper.

For weeks after I take off the uniform, something keeps me in, keeps me silent. I have yet to escape a sense of duty about the army, a sense of what I should and shouldn't stand for as a representation of the modern soldier. It's also fear that keeps me in. Irrational fear, really. Fear that I'll lose my veterans benefits. Fear that I'll be pulled back in. Fear related to years of hearing my peers and my bosses talk about how they'd kick a soldier's ass (or worse) if they knew he was gay. I've yet to repair the injury caused by being fearful for years that I would, at best, be asked to leave, that I would be told that I don't belong.

In December 2010, only a few people in my office know that I date women. I've been seeing the same woman for a few years now, but here in this gay office in D.C., everyone assumes I mean boyfriend or husband when I say *partner*.

When I came back out earlier this year, I did so in the most theatrical of ways. (Although it is hard to call it a coming out; no one suspected I was straight at that point.) The day I formally got out of the military, the day the ink dried, the day any real risk in doing so disappeared, gay blogs across the country shared a letter that I wrote to the President, calling for the end of the law called "Don't Ask, Don't Tell." In the letter, I come out as bisexual again, and I brag about my silent service.

Honestly, at this point, I'm not sure that *bisexual* is the right word. There is this ongoing in-group conversation about whether or not the term reinforces a gender binary, so *queer*, or *pansexual* might be better terms to describe me being into people of every gender. Because the letter is a rhetorical act, a marketing ploy aimed at a general audience, I keep it simple.

In December 2009, before I go, I'm not exactly *passing* for heterosexual. In uniform I am not a towering presence. I have a slight lisp and overly groomed eyebrows. I often forgo the required beret in my uniform because I don't want to mess up my hair. I don't hide that I've got a gay job lined up in D.C. In this hyper-masculine, heteronormative culture, I stand out.

I'm also the noncommissioned officer assigned to lecture my unit on the regulations regarding sexual harassment, equal opportunity, and the current policy restricting open service for gay and lesbian troops in the military. This isn't punishment or an inappropriate joke on the part of my bosses; I volunteered for this position.

The last presentation I gave on these subjects wasn't much different from the rest. A few dozen troops in their uniforms packed into a classroom as I flipped through a slideshow presentation.

"The goal of the Army's Equal Opportunity policy is to ensure fair treatment of all soldiers." I tell them again, the same mandatory message they heard last quarter and the quarter before.

When the part on "Don't Ask, Don't Tell" comes up, I feel the room get quieter. I feel it as a stillness on my skin, as if these warriors were holding their breath. Or not. The truth is, very few soldiers really gave much consideration to the rule. Even in this conservative culture, most of the people who have work to do every day don't seem to care anymore. It's a non-issue these days. It is as likely as not that any tension in the air during these sessions was imagined by a soldier with a lot on his shoulders.

"There is no constitutional right to serve in the armed forces," I tell them, reading from the slide. "The presence in the armed forces of persons who demonstrate a propensity or intent to engage in homosexual acts would create an unacceptable risk to the high standards of morale, good order and discipline, and unit cohesion that are the essence of military capability."

I don't mind saying it. It's not masochism; it's relief of pressure, the chance to talk about it, the chance to speak.

★

In December 2010, I am still keeping my hair short on the sides, although now I grow it into a wide, Mohawk-type mess on the top. I'm wearing dress shirts and ties for the first time in my life, but because this is a trendy, modern office (trendy for D.C., at least), I'm not in a suit. Jeans and a button-up aren't out of place here. On Fridays, when it gets casual, I wear a T-shirt, which shows the collection of tattoos I amassed while serving.

Short sleeves in the office bring about another first—being considered butch.

"So you got all your tattoos when you were in the Army?" a member of the field team—the attractive men and women who go out to get petitions signed—asks me, as he leans onto my desk and lifts the sleeve of my shirt.

"I love guys with tattoos," he says as he smiles before strutting away.

Here in this culture, where everyone is assumed gay first, my tattoos, my novice sense of style, and my history in the military present me as almost a tough guy. A little bit butch. Probably a top.

In December 2009, I am a superhero.

When soldiers tell people, at least people who live on and around military bases, that they train dogs for the army, there are only a few responses that they get.

That is so cool. Wow. How did you get into that? So you get to play with dogs every day?

When we're hanging out in our office, with our dogs kenneled nearby, barking to each other, K-9 handlers pretend to complain, pretend as though we tire of this routine. We don't. We love the vest with *K-9* printed on the back that we wear over our fatigues. We love parking anywhere we please and keeping the oversize SUVs running because we have to keep our eyes on the dogs. We love wrapping our leashes around our shoulders, or letting them hang off of our belts, so that everyone can see them. We like silently encouraging people to ask.

It's the attention. It's the fact that we're being zipped around the world to search for bombs, the fact that we're rubbing elbows with Secret Service in NYC. This feels like rock star status. It's among the reasons that so few handlers are in a rush to leave the military.

"What is it that you think you are you going to do when you get out?" the First Sergeant often asks soldiers to scare them from leaving.

In December 2010, I am a lackey.

My boss is significantly more butch than I am. No, not butch—he wears polo shirts tight enough to cling to his chest and arms—but aggressive. From my cubicle outside of his office, I watch as my coworkers leave conversations with him muttering under their breath, almost crying sometimes. He doesn't budge. He gets his way.

"Listen, my friend." One can tell he has distaste for someone when he calls them *friend*. "That just isn't going to happen."

My job, the job I left the army for, the job for which I went to school at night while serving in K-9 units across the globe, is to keep him happy. Expense reports. Travel arrangements. Find him a place that ships suits. Call him a taxi.

"Anthony," he calls from his desk, not bothering to stand. "How about a cupcake run?" Cupcakes for the whole office, on him. (Expensed to the organization, but at least it's him who asks me to make the order, to walk down to the boutique bakery to pick up our treats).

And here's the thing, as much as this sounds like whining, I wear a genuine smile as I stand in the brightly lit bakery in Dupont Circle, the historically gay district of the city, in tight slacks and a shirt pinned closed with a skinny tie, balancing several bright pink boxes of three-dollar-apiece cupcakes to hand out to an office full of happy, queer professionals.

In December 2009, I say *K-9*. I say *SSD. SSG. LP/OP. QRF.* We say *FOB*, even *fobbit. K-pot. CAB. 550 cord. 9 mil. Downrange. FRAGO. XO. BOLO. IED. CBRN* or *NBC. RPG. Sham-shield. Stripes. NCOIC. MWR. MRE. DFAC. FTX. PX. M249 Getsome, Getsome.*

★

In December 2010, I say *sexual orientation*. I say *LGBT*. Try *LGBTIQQAA2-S*. I say *HRC. NCTE. NCLR. HIV/AIDS. Whitman-Walker. Kinsey. Butler. Sexual orientation. Gender identity. Gender expression. Gender nonconforming. Second-parent adoption. Medical power-of-attorney. Civil union. SSM. MSM. GLADD* and single-D *GLAD, NCOD, ENDA, DADT, DOMA. Repeal, Repeal.*

In December 2009, Staff Sergeant Burrell, the married, straight soldier who presents the equal opportunity lectures with me, stands with me in uniform in the hallway of my unit headquarters before I walk out the door for the last time. Without any hush in his voice, he asks me the most personal question he is permitted to ask me.

"Do you think that they'll repeal it within your lifetime?"

"My lifetime? Of course, two or three more years of this, tops."

"I'm not so sure, there are plenty of old crusty types who are going to bitch about it."

I nod. "Yeah, but it's not them who gets to decide. This is going down. We've got a campaign promise."

He lets a smirk creep out, not a mischievous one, not exactly. It is something closer to the smile of someone getting away with something, a whispered *ask*. "I half-hoped it would be repealed before you went."

I blush. Despite his benign intent, despite my reemerging pride, I feel as though I am being accused of something. This should be the moment in which I come out, at least to a soldier I trust, when the stakes are low.

I don't.

★

In December 2010, I am sitting in a meeting space on the first floor of building where I work in D.C. The space here is all glass and milky white surfaces, floor-to-ceiling windows, plenty of light.

Today there are rows of chairs and a projection screen set up for us, for those of us who aren't down the street watching firsthand the President sign this bill into law.

I've been misty-eyed all day. I could barely keep it together on the subway train in, so I know that I might lose it when the livestream starts. I sit in the back with a cup of coffee, my legs crossed as I lean forward at the edge of my seat. I've got a lot on my to-do list today: expense reports, blog posts, a celebratory cupcake run, no doubt. Still, today they will cut me some slack. As the stream begins, we watch on the projectors as the camera scans the crowd. The gay congressman is there. There's the Arabic linguist whom the army asked to leave, and the pilot kicked out just before retirement. There's Eric, who lost his leg during the first push into Iraq.

"Hey, Anthony," a blond coworker with a sweet face and kind, blue eyes sits down beside me in a T-shirt that reads REPEAL THE BAN. "Didn't you used to be in the military?"

"Yeah," I tell him, beginning to smile. "Used to."

Somewhere along the line, my feelings about queer folks serving in the military will get blurry. I'll start realizing how, even as it was a ladder out of poverty for me, I can't say whether I believe in what we were doing. Soon I'll recognize that, as many times as the U.S. military has been sent in to be the superheroes, some men in suits have sent us to do something ugly. Maybe it's the seemingly unending wars of the start of the twenty-first century, or maybe it's just me coming to terms with being had, being sold a narrative that's only half true, but the vision I have of my military service is starting to crack, and those cracks are starting to show.

I smile with some resignation, keeping my eyes on the screen as they well up. I smile with a small amount of embarrassment, with a small amount of pride. As the morning sun slips in through the window behind my seat, I smile, out of uniform.

"Thank you. Thank you," the President begins. "Today is a good day."

GOING OUT

Seventeen. Reno, Nevada
"Why would anybody want . . ."

My fake ID says that I am twenty. I am the only person that I know, or will ever know, who has a fake ID that says younger than twenty-one.

I use the fake ID to get into dance clubs during eighteen-and-up nights at the only spot I know of in the city that young people go to dance to anything other than country music.

I have never used it to get into a gay club. The gay club is still a myth to me. A foreign idea. At this age, it is a frightening place that people sneak in and out of: a Masonic hall filled with veteran disciples of a secret society who would devastate a neophyte like me.

Nineteen and a long way from home. Seoul, Republic of Korea
"You're an American soldier, yes?"

They do not ask to see an ID to get into gay clubs in here. They ask for fifteen thousand won, which my trembling hands exchange for entry and two drink tickets.

I use the drink tickets, glossy coupons with the name of the club—Why Not?—printed upon them, for vodka and tonic, which I quickly determine to be undrinkable, but that I continue to sip because it is what others are ordering.

I have closely trimmed hair that gives me away as an American soldier. Among the crowd of Koreans, expat English teachers, and business travelers from all over, we stand out with tight haircuts and a distinctly youthful American style. An outdated law forces the troops into silence, but as the night gets blurrier and the eye contact gets more intense, we similarly groomed Americans will begin to flirt with one another.

Actually twenty. San Antonio, Texas

"My friend thinks that you are really cute."

Certain clubs here are off-limits for personnel assigned to the 241st training squadron; the reason listed in our handbook is "numerous reports of illicit drug use," but it's because they can't just say "gay bar."

I use the handbook to locate these bars on Friday and Saturday nights. Danyel joins me for these adventures. The year prior we both sat in gunner platforms atop the Humvees of second squad, fourth platoon, of the 57th Military Police Company; now we break the ice for each other in these bars, and if it ever came down to it, we would pretend to be the other's date in a bind. The two of us visit glammed-up dives with neon lights and dark corners, where I see drag for the first time and blush when I am hit on by older men.

I have an ID that says I am twenty-five, although I'm told by the older men that I look seventeen.

Twenty-two. Fort Irwin, California

"I don't have a roommate, would you like to come to my place?"

There are no gay clubs here on the lonely military base isolated in a high desert of the West. There are nods and looks and subtle signs at parties that lead to brief and intense necking in the rooms of Military Police barracks.

I use these secretive, sloppy sessions and a sticker on the back of a purple Ford hatchback to claim my identity within a Queer community from which I am cut off. I have a whispered reputation as "that gay MP" whom my supervisors wish they could do away with.

Twenty-seven. Washington, District of Columbia
"Where do you work?"

The gayborhood here is just down the road from where lobbyists and lawyers run the country. I cannot afford to live here, so I stay outside of the city.

I use my new job working for a gay rights organization to try to blend into a crowd that wears business-casual while talking about legislation and the Real Housewives.

I feel out of place in pricey and crowded gay bars overflowing with pomp, but being partnered and now considering myself something close to a grownup, I'm convinced that I would rather be here discussing policy than at the queer dancehall down the street filled with shirtless boys who look like they are seventeen with IDs that say they are twenty-five.

Twenty-eight. Baltimore, Maryland
"I used to be stationed nearby too. Which branch?"

The folks in gay bars here aren't concerned with what you do for a living, especially on Show Tunes Night, and the bartenders don't care whether you are straight or gay or pansexual, especially on Monday nights, when the bar is otherwise empty.

I use the connections that I've made in this community to write for a local gay newspaper, where my name appears in print above my words and behind a cover emblazoned with the words GAY LIFE.

I have a feeling of being home for the first time in a long time. The bars here, like the city, aren't perfect, but they are comfortable. Every now and then, I'll catch a look from a young man with a tight haircut and a distinctly youthful American style, and I'll say hi and do my best to explain to him where I am from.

PHOTO: PRIDE, 2011

MICHELLE is the one who looks like a frat boy, the one with the sideways ball cap and T-shirt. She always wore her hair long like this, but still carried a certain butchness with her, her military service always showing just a bit, no matter the setting. That year she had flown in from overseas just for the Pride parade, catching a flight from some Nordic country to this enduring East Coast city that her queer chosen family calls home. In a T-shirt and cargo shorts, she seems carefree, a tipsy smirk just starting to shine through.

On the other side of me is Elizabeth, her toned, black arms behind us, pulling us all in to huddle for the photo. Four years after the photo, when we all get the call, I won't see Elizabeth for months. I hear that she took it hard, but the distance is my fault—I wasn't ready to mourn publicly for the funeral, nor for the informal reception that followed in the gayborhood, the same neighborhood that acts as our backdrop here in the photo. Mt. Vernon is a skyline of early-century rowhomes crisscrossed by fire escapes and accented with the steady hum of car traffic. It is the home of Baltimore's Pride celebration and the bars where this group of lesbians introduced me to queer city life.

We were all friends, but Elizabeth and Michelle were conjoined, de facto sisters and best friends who everyone believed were in love with each other. They were, but not in the way those who knew them guessed. More than their girlfriends, more than Michelle's brothers- and sisters-in-arms, probably as much as their families, Michelle and Elizabeth loved each other with an understanding and loyalty that was fierce and unyielding. They each loved the women they dated, and they had to insist all the time that they weren't secretly dating or sleeping with each other, but it wasn't an attraction between them. It was love.

Ann Marie is on the edge of the huddle. Being a queer woman who dated people of any gender, and joining our group later than everyone else, she felt hesitant the first time she came to Pride. She worried that lesbians would tell her she wasn't gay enough, that she didn't belong at a celebration like ours, in this downtown parking lot with dance music blaring from the cabins of new trucks and Jeeps and half-dressed women making out more and more sloppily as the day's drinks piled up. But Michelle made sure Ann Marie felt like a part of it all, made sure that she was invited to drinks at Sappho's, to Pride parades, to join the group of middle-age cops, lawyers, artists, and soldiers for dinners and brunches.

That's me in the center, the guy, the one with the tipsy smile stretching from one side of my round face to another. A couple of years out of the military, I am wearing a scruff on my face and a messy mohawk under a cap. It being Pride, I am drunk, just short of messy on Gatorade spiked with soju. Despite my gender, I am welcome here, in the parking lot of gay and bi women dancing and drinking outside of their trucks and their Jeeps, a beer pong and an ice luge set up in the aisles between cars. Michelle introduced me to this scene when I landed here in Maryland, when we were both stationed nearby, me just newly returned to the U.S. She was the one who showed me the bars and clubs here. This is her Pride; the group is her gang, strong Out women who know how to be queer urbanites.

That's how it was for us, queer misfits who found each other despite the silence. Somehow, my hushed signals were picked up, and our quiet nods were acknowledged, and I was in. Drinks at the lesbian bar, tailgating in the parking lot, familial gestures that said: *This is our queer city, and now it is your queer city. Welcome home.* Eventually Michelle will move, and I'll leave the military, but we will each uncover members of the tribe elsewhere, even as we moved onward. Eventually, Michelle will find her way home to Pittsburgh, and into the arms of a woman who loves her, who supports her emotionally as she deals with the transition from a jet-set life protecting military generals throughout Europe to a life in college classrooms full of students Michelle calls children—this is the transition from hero to veteran, a champion of yesterday.

I don't know why she did it. Maybe it was the transition, or maybe something she hid beneath the surface. Maybe it was a bright red scream she wanted the whole world to hear, or maybe she just couldn't take another day.

When you get this, call me. It's important. It's Michelle.

We're all grinning in the photo, proud smiles, drunk smiles. We're all joyful to be reunited for a moment. It's one of our last moments all together like this, all in one place. It wasn't this Baltimore she came back to, not Mt. Vernon, this strange neighborhood where Gertrude Stein and Emily Post both once lived. It was Pittsburgh she returned to, close to family, close to school, close to Angie, who lasted for a couple of years. It was the Pittsburgh Veterans Affairs hospital she returned to, where she saw a counselor for a while who helped with the transition. It was Pittsburgh she returned to for school, graduating from one university and working security for another, a bright pupil who everyone said was heading in the right direction. It was Pittsburgh she left from, in a car, in the veterans hospital parking lot. Michelle was a veteran, one of twenty-two leaving that way every day.

SISTERS IN THE PRESENCE OF STRANGERS, PT. II

THE PARADOX of the Queer story is pride. Western queer literature is nothing new—it's found in our mythologies, it's found in Homer, it's certainly found in Sappho—but in the twentieth century, this literature has a habit of moving between the joy of recognition and the pain of shame. The history of the West is that of a world that aims to destroy and erase queer people, so it may follow that our literature explores the shattering that happens in such a world, as well as the pride of surviving. Part of Snediker's project is to move beyond the stories of queer shame (HIV/AIDS, familial dishonor, suicide) that the end of the millennium left us with. The truth is somewhere in between though. That's the paradox. Our joy, our pride, our possibilities: they arrive through survival, through finding some chosen family on the other side of increased rates of suicide, addiction, homelessness, eating disorders. If we are a people (and there are folks out there who would argue that we are not a people) it is because we have found each other in the dark. The light we find is important, but we would take it for granted if not for that darkness.

Dany

"Tony!" Danyel shouted over the bacchanal that swelled all around her. She called my name out through the tacky July heat the parade moved through, over the shirtless dancers and the papier mâché rainbows, through the roar of butch women on motorcycles and cheer risen for the parents with the "I love my trans son" signs. It had been years since I had seen her, our second time in Korea, before she deployed to the desert and I came toward D.C. The last time we saw each other, both were still as closeted as we could stand, but both of us had whispers swirling around us.

There, just north of Dupont Circle, surrounded by twinks and queens and bears and butches, we were not closeted. We found each other with a sticky embrace, covered in the day's sweat, and glitter, and stickers, and temporary tattoos of rainbows and equals signs.

"How are you? What are you doing?" she yelled over the music.

"Drinking and flirting! Same as you."

We caught up with each other's lives, her about to start medical school, I about to finish a master's degree in writing. Her with a husband back home, me with my girlfriend and her girlfriend beside me there at the parade. Neither of us carried much regret about leaving, about racing away from the machine that tried to eat us up.

Later we will tell each other how much we meant to each other, how I helped her realize who she was, and she helped me survive, helped me keep my shit together through the toxic masculinity of military service, but for now, we don't need any of that. That old ritual, being drunk at Pride, is what we need. It shouldn't mean as much to us as it does, but here we are, sweaty and drunk and nearly in tears as we spend a few moments together out in the open, in the summer sunlight, joyful and queer.

Bea

"I need to get out of here right now."

"Are you okay? Do you need some water?"

"Like, right fucking now."

Bea never said what it was that brought her back like this—not broken, that isn't something a veteran is, but always at the edge of herself, a rubber band pulled tauter than it should be. In a dump of a seafood restaurant, barely standing between the north- and south-bound lanes of a highway a couple of hours from the sea, I think it was something about the smell that got to her. We had come for crabs, the local delicacy of her new home here in Maryland, and the scent greeted us as soon as we stepped in. Wafting over the checkered tablecloths, the scent of fish and crab and blistering oil hit us as soon as we swung open the jingling door. It lingered as we ordered and sat down in the folding chairs. It was once we sat that I noticed Bea shifting about. She kept looking around. Her hands kept shaking. That's when she told me she needed to leave.

She bolted out of the door after she told me. Leaving the new guy she was seeing at the table, along with her expensive new sunglasses, the keys to her Jeep, her flip phone.

"Should I . . ."

"I'll go see what's up."

Outside in the gravel parking lot, she was already pacing and holding back tears.

"I don't know if it was that kid screeching or the horrible smell, I just needed to get out of there."

"Do you want to go?"

"I don't know."

"Do you want a hug?"

"I don't want anyone to touch me right now."

"Do you want me to go back inside?"

"Just—just stay here for a moment."

I stayed. Bea cried. Big tears, the type that cause that ugly gasping sound. Tears that didn't know exactly where they came from, maybe relief of being home, maybe fear of being home. Maybe a memory of something from Over There, maybe a memory of someone. She never told me, she just cried, and I just stood there near her, in a parking lot between the lanes of a highway, while our soft-shelled crabs got cold.

Michelle

"It's been too long!"

"For sure. Let me know when you're in town again. We'd love to see you."

"For sure. :) Thanks again."

That was the last conversation that I can confirm I had with her. I know that we spoke later that summer, that I saw her at Baltimore's Pride festival, just as I did every year. I know that we were both probably drunk, that, then too, we would have said that it had been too long, and that that summer would be the one I would finally make it up to Pittsburgh. There's no record of that conversation though—social media doesn't save your entire life for posterity, just the bright spots. All that remained was a brief, utilitarian online chat about a job reference and catching up soon, a moment saved for perpetuity.

Ten months after the message, it would have been a seasonably mild day in the suburbs on the north end of Pittsburgh. Just north of the Allegheny River and the Allegheny Expressway and the suburban strip mall with a Ross and a burger joint named Burgatory, Michelle would have been one of hundreds of veterans across generations visiting the H. J. Heinz Campus of the Pittsburgh Veterans Affairs Medical System. At some point, the veteran of the U.S. war in Afghanistan would have traveled along a road named Patriot Way. At some point, she would have parked in one of the sprawling campus' multi-row parking lots and gone in for an appointment at the center, passing young veterans like herself as well as old men with post-service paunches and snapback hats emblazoned with the name of their war as she entered one of the hospital's bright new buildings, buildings built in response to the swell of returning veterans from America's longest war and the needs of aging veterans of the wars of the twentieth century.

Dozens must have seen her leave her appointment a short time later, stepping out from the office to the bright lobby, the lobby into the crisp air, the trees still bare, but the weather offering a hint that the promise of spring seemed just around the corner. One or two folks must have seen her as she marched across the parking lot, where the trucks and cars were stuck with purple heart license plates and wounded warrior stickers. I wonder who was there to see her as she slipped into her car. I wonder if they knew that twenty-two veterans kill themselves every day in America. I wonder if anyone who saw her knew that lesbian and bisexual women are more than twice as likely to attempt suicide than their heterosexual counterparts. All the time I think about the moment she must have slammed shut her car door, the moment she reached into the glove box, where she kept a pistol. I wonder if she would have had it loaded, or if she fumbled through sliding bullets into the magazine, the magazine into the gun, before the moment she raised it to her skull and ended her life.

PHOTO: WESTWARD

IN THE black and white photo, I am looking over a body of water, and its vastness might lure you into believing it is the sea. Because this is the end of the book, you might be convinced that I am on the western coast, the symbol for endless possibility, the direction toward which the wild move, where the sun ends its journey each day.

It's easy to mistake the cropping of rocks between me and the un-sea as the 7,600 miles of western coastline where the nation throws itself at the Pacific. The stones are pocked and unruly, otherworldly like the West.

One doesn't see my entire face, just a profile with eyeglasses and a softened chin, hair close, but not meticulous. These details reveal that I am not old, but I am no longer the youth who ran off to see the world, who clenched his fist and dashed off when the call to war rang like a fire alarm in a going-nowhere town.

But it isn't the Pacific I'm gazing toward; those rocks aren't the spot where the continent meets the Ring of Fire. Here I'm traveling across the nation, east to west, but I haven't yet met the sea. I'm standing on the southern tip of the Great Salt Lake, still hundreds of miles, two long days worth of driving, from the ocean. I'm standing somewhere near the middle of my journey, somewhere just past the center of the country, just over the continental divide. I'm headed west, convinced that it might still be home, not the sage and the pine of Nevada, but home where I was born, the Golden State. There is another graduate school there, and a chance to teach, and the chance to put my feet back into the sea and let the sun go each evening.

D.C. was a bust. The polish and posturing didn't fit right for a runaway. I left it to pick up a pen, to get a degree in writing, to learn to teach. I left to Baltimore, a city that that everyone forgets over and over again, until it bursts like one of Hughes' fiery dreams. I fall in love. I write for papers. I get a graduate degree. Baltimore welcomes everyone who washes up on its shore, it always has, from Edgar Allan Poe to F. Scott Fitzgerald. It's a town that's been left out in the rain, but still finds new life, like lichens clung to concrete.

I take it for granted. Wrap it all up and leave the city, and a nice job at a university, and a thriving arts scene, and a chosen family of queer folks, lost boys and girls who found comfort leaning our backs against each other. Each day before I leave, I try to talk another friend into packing up and coming with me, running away with me to the sunshine and salt water. I tell them about the lack of seasons, about the air near the Monterey Bay, where one can stand on the cliffs and watch whales and otter socialize. They ask about earthquakes, about the drought, about the cost of living, but the truth is that this isn't about California; it's about Baltimore. Baltimore feels like your favorite comforter, home, even as it begins to show signs of wear.

The Great Salt Lake isn't the ocean though; it isn't limitless. The lake is landlocked, more in-between places than a place itself. The area surrounding the lake was settled by Americans in the 1840s only because a religious figure led a group of Mormon exiles out of the eastern U.S., refugees searching for a somewhere to call their own. Before then, long before then—before the Mormons, before the Donner

Party passed through, before the Shoshone, Paiute, and the Goshute called the area home—the lake was much greater, ten times the Great Lake's current size. Time has transformed the region, radically shifted the features once essential. All that remains of that vastness are sprawling plains of salt that look like the surface of the moon in the summertime.

It is autumn in the photo. Within a few months, the salt flats will bear a thin layer of water that make them appear as a mirror that extends for miles toward the hills. We're not there yet though: September is one of those in-between periods, summer slowly retreating and the cool air just beginning to whisper of the cold to come. In the east, the change is dramatic—out west, it is a mere hum. Here in the middle of somewhere, between seasons, everything feels like the moment between inhale and exhale.

My look to the west isn't terminal. It's just a stop on a journey to the sea. I didn't come here for the lake, the lake just happened to be where I ended another long day of driving toward something new. In the late morning, I pull into a lot on the southern tip, where the great serpent of Interstate 80 grazes the lake. At first the stop feels almost like an annoyance, an unneeded luxury distracting me from the long drive remaining. Slowly though, the moonscape overtakes me, suspends me in the in-between that forgets the relentless turn of the clock.

"Have you ever seen anything like it?" my companion asks of the lake after she snaps the photo.

"No. This is all brand-new to me."

NOTES

"Dulce et decorum est pro patria mori" is a line from Horace's *Odes*, and has appeared in numerous works since.

The line "Get Busy Living or Get Busy Dying" is quoted from the film *Shawshank Redemption*.

The line "peers and leaders who betray expectations in egregious ways" is quoted from *Moral Injury in the Context of War* by Shira Maguen, PhD, and Brett Litz, PhD.

The essay "Headlines from the *Reno-Gazette Journal* the Morning of September 11, 2001" is made entirely of the headlines of the daily newspaper in Reno, Nevada.

In "Wrong as Two Boys," I directly quote USC Code 10 Section 654.

The quoted lines "an uninterrupted line, extended from the target to the muzzle, down the sights to the buttstock, from the rifle to the shoulder, straight down to your boots" and "inhale and exhale naturally, firing during the natural respiratory pause at the bottom of the exhale" are taken from TRADOC Pamphlet 600–4.

The line "Psychologists know that this kind of powerful 'operant conditioning' is the only technique which will reliably influence the primitive midbrain processing of a frightened human being" is directly quoted from "Psychological Effects of Combat" by Dave Grossman and Bruce K. Siddle.

Throughout "Great Basin," I use lines from popular U.S. Army cadence calls.

"A clean break is something you cannot come back from; that is irretrievable because it makes the past cease to exist" is quoted from F. Scott Fitzgerald's essay "The Crack Up."

"Their refusal to do so will result in military conflict, commenced at a time of our choosing" is a direct quote from President Bush's speech on March 17, 2003.

"I want you to remember that no bastard ever won a war by dying for his country. He won it by making the other poor, dumb bastard die for his country" is a direct quote from the 1970 film *Patton*.

The description for "inspection arms" is quoted directly from Army Field Manual 3–21.5.

"CHEONG-JU CITY HARDCORE" is a line from the song "CJCH" by 13steps.

"It's intimidating at first," Moll said. "It's a high-stress situation" and "The installation recognized some of its finest Soldiers in a ceremony Friday at garrison head-quarters" are quoted from an October 2008 issue of the Fort Meade *Soundoff!*

In the section of "Dogs of War" subtitled "2008—U.S. Occupied Iraq," I describe a video shared nationally in 2008/2009, and quote the dialogue directly.

In other sections of "Dogs of War," I directly quote Army Field Manual 3–19.17 and Army Regulation 190–12, and I describe the findings of Philip Zimbardo's TED Talk, "The Psychology of Evil."

THE JOURNAL NON/FICTION PRIZE

(formerly The Ohio State University Prize in Short Fiction)

Out of Step: A Memoir
ANTHONY MOLL

Brief Interviews with the Romantic Past
KATHRYN NUERNBERGER

Landfall: A Ring of Stories
JULIE HENSLEY

Hibernate
ELIZABETH ESLAMI

The Deer in the Mirror
CARY HOLLADAY

How
GEOFF WYSS

Little America
DIANE SIMMONS

The Book of Right and Wrong
MATT DEBENHAM

The Departure Lounge: Stories and a Novella
PAUL EGGERS

True Kin
RIC JAHNA

Owner's Manual
MORGAN MCDERMOTT

Mexico Is Missing: And Other Stories
J. DAVID STEVENS

Ordination
SCOTT A. KAUKONEN

Little Men: Novellas and Stories
GERALD SHAPIRO

The Bones of Garbo
    TRUDY LEWIS

The White Tattoo: A Collection of Short Stories
    WILLIAM J. COBB

Come Back Irish
    WENDY RAWLINGS

Throwing Knives
    MOLLY BEST TINSLEY

Dating Miss Universe: Nine Stories
    STEVEN POLANSKY

Radiance: Ten Stories
    JOHN J. CLAYTON